THE *Waiting* GAME

Future Best
Publishing

PRAISE FOR "THE WAITING GAME"

I have been privileged to grow up with Sister Yimi—or as the world knows her, Olayimika Awujoola—as one of my greatest role models who has shaped me into the woman I am today. She is someone who not only provides an abundance of joy and happiness to others, but shares endless wisdom that is based on the Lord's understanding rather than her own. I have been fortunate to see her *big* acts of faith and obedience in trusting the Lord, along with the fruits of this. She inspires me to trust in the ways of God in *all* things.

The message that God has given her to share within *The Waiting Game* is necessary and important for all believers. It is tailored to help people, no matter their circumstances. This book has opened my eyes to the importance of the waiting period and made me more excited and intrigued to know and learn the ways of God. If you are in a waiting period and feeling discouraged or alone, this book is for you! Olayimika beautifully shares her moments of pain and challenges that were transformed into the very purpose that will give you hope to stay aligned with God's plan for your life.

— FAVOR OLOWOKERE

I read *The Waiting Game* within a day, as I couldn't put it down. I was filled with many emotions as I read, but the best was the personal confirmation I received that God still has me in mind and has a great future planned for me. The book helped me to shift my thinking and provided great insight on how I can develop myself while I continue to trust God for my blessings. While the author narrated her story about waiting for her God-ordained husband, I was able to tap into her testimonies and apply them to my waiting period wholeheartedly.

Anyone who has been waiting on something and growing weary needs to pick up this book and begin reading. This book is confirmation that God is still in the business of doing miracles, and that what God cannot do, absolutely doesn't exist! *The Waiting Game* is truly a faith-booster and a hope-lifter for anyone trusting God for a particular miracle.

— MIMI

As I sit here writing this testimony, I want to start by saying how thankful I am to have been able to spend the past five years with Yimi! She is one of the most beautiful people I have known. And her beauty lies in her honesty, creativeness, loyalty, and kindness. Even though I come from a different religion, Yimi made me believe and see Jesus in a whole new light. Her encouragement to follow in the word of the Lord let me have complete trust and faith in our loving Father at the right time. I believe He knew I would be in need at that time, and He sent Yimi to show me the way.

When Yimi told me about her endeavors to write a book, I felt God placed this intention for a reason. He knew she would enlighten many people through her stories and writing.

Five years later, I have grown my faith in Christ by praying every day and giving my cares, happiness, and struggles to God.

— PRIYANKA RAVULA

THE *Waiting* GAME

*Staying in **FAITH** as you align yourself with God's plan.*

Olayimika Awujoola

Future Best
PUBLISHING

To my darling husband—the first person to read this book from cover to cover—for supporting, inspiring, and motivating me through it all. You have never doubted my ability to do anything. You cheer me on and speak only positive words over me. Without you, I'd have no story! I love you.

To my daughter, my little president, a true champion, Iréoluwa Ivana. I see God's love and goodness daily through you. You are God's masterpiece. You inspire your mommy to be the best version of herself. I love you immensely, my darling daughter.

To my future child...you are fearfully and wonderfully made by God. I love you dearly and await you in Jesus's name.

CONTENTS

INTRODUCTION

Do you have a goal, a brewing idea, or a perfect picture of how you would like your life to look at a certain point, but none of it seems to be working out? Or have you drawn up a plan, set the work in motion, and the dreams still feel far out of reach? For years, my answer to that was, "Yes!"

We are often expected to have a planned destination for our life's journey. People may ask about our short- or long-term goals; our one-, five-, or ten-year plan; or just what we are hoping to achieve. Many see this planning as part of what defines us, or as evidence that a person has matured and become responsible. The Bible says, "Write the vision, and make it plain upon tablets, that he may run that readeth it" (Habakkuk 2:2 KJV).

Among my many goals, plans, and visions, one stood out to me for years as most important, the determination to be married —and to marry well according to God's standards. I was privileged to discover some of God's purposes for my life at a young age, one of which was to help people form healthy, Godly, and enjoyable Christian relationships and marriages. That concept is almost foreign in our society today. I did not have any good examples while growing up, and that made me even more determined to get this aspect of my life right and do it God's way. To fully manifest this purpose, I believed I needed to be married or at least be in a relationship. As the years went by, however, my husband remained far out of sight.

In my final year of high school, I had my entire life nicely figured out, or so I believed. I lived in Lagos, Nigeria, but was born in the US—in Boston, Massachusetts—and was taken to Nigeria as an infant. My plan was to move back to the United States after High School and study pharmacy, then return to Nigeria, serve in the National Youth Service Corps (NYSC), open a pharmacy in Nigeria, and be swept off my feet and married to my Prince Charming by age twenty-three. I would have three kids by age twenty-five and perhaps a fourth by age thirty. My plans ended there.

It felt good to have goals I was working towards. I saw the big picture and was certain I had orchestrated a beautiful life's journey for myself. I wouldn't say I asked God if all of these steps were in accordance with his plan and will for my life, but I do recall praying, "God, please let me get into pharmacy school," "God, please bring the bone of my bones," and so on.

I was living by this timetable until I began to realize that it takes more than just making plans and putting a schedule in place to have or accomplish all that I desired. Things took a different turn. For example, I did not pass one of the main courses I needed in order to be considered for pharmacy school. I repeated it a few times, but my grade did not improve. I had no idea where my life was headed.

What happened to all my plans, goals, and dreams? My career path completely changed. I am not a pharmacist today. I never went back to Nigeria to serve the country. And my biggest dream of being married at twenty-three? I didn't connect with anyone. It just did not happen—not at twenty-three, twenty-four, or even twenty-five.

The clock was ticking, but other areas of my life began to take shape. Not, of course, how I'd planned. Still, I was very happy with the turn my life was taking. My academics and new career finally began going smoothly, I felt stable financially, and I had the most enjoyable journey with God. Everything but the marriage bit took an admirable form. I got closer and closer to thirty, and I was still waiting.

All of this and more showed me that, "Many are the plans in a person's heart, but it is the Lord's purpose that prevails" (Proverbs 19:21 NIV). I learned to cope with the reality that setting goals and designing timelines for myself independently was not working. I needed to be in alignment with and dependent on God for any plans to fall into place.

After this realization, I determined to make the best of my waiting period. I got comfortable with the wait, started to enjoy it, in fact. The fire of faith so consumed me; I knew without a single doubt that my wait could not be in vain. I would be married, and to a good man. My marriage would be like that between Christ and the church. That would be worth the waiting.

I became more particular about God's plan, timing, and specifications for the spouse he intended for me. More importantly, I focused on what I needed to do *while* I waited. After all, I needed to play my part as I stayed confident that this wait would pay off. And boy, oh boy, I was bountifully compensated.

The Waiting Game is a faith-booster that tells the story of how God took me through a series of interesting events, and—in a way and time I absolutely did not expect—blessed me with the fulfillment of my dream. A husband, and a fantastic one at that! God made me the living evidence of what only he, the Almighty, can do.

I believe I owe it to you—and anyone else trusting God for something, no matter how big or small—to share the story of how God took all of my plans, put them in a bag, and stirred up faith in me to totally surrender to *his* plan and purpose for my life. I cannot over-emphasize how important the application of faith was to that process.

This book will walk you through the journey of my highs and lows, as well as the measures I took, types of prayers I prayed, and things I did or did not do during my waiting period. It also highlights some persecutions I faced for my application of faith, but it demonstrates the true joy of knowing that God's plan for me—and for you—always has been and always will be nothing short of spectacular.

My prayer is that faith will be renewed in the heart of every reader, you will be encouraged and propelled to not just "write the vision and make it plain" but to write a vision that aligns with God's plan and purpose for your life.

Believe with every ounce of faith in you that "[...] the vision is yet for an appointed time, but at the end it shall speak, and not lie: though it tarry, wait for it; because it will surely come, it will not tarry" (Habakkuk 2:3 KJV). The wait eventually pays. God paid me!

CHAPTER 1

EXPECTATIONS

How many times has someone advised you to write down your goals? Perhaps you've heard this at work as part of your career development, in school at the beginning of a new semester, or even at church on New Year's Eve. At some point in life, we realize we just need to set goals—short-term, long-term, personal, career, financial, health, weight, dating, marriage, business—and the list goes on. Many experts say these goals need to be SMART (Specific, Measurable, Attainable, Relevant, and Time-Based). Makes sense, but all this can become a bit overwhelming, right?

My reality with goal-setting was a bit different. I believed I had set clear goals, and I was right, but it took me a while to realize I was just following the societal standards I'd been exposed to. I needed to go to school, graduate, then get some more education and probably strive to become a doctor. If that was too farfetched, I needed to at least get a master's degree with continued education. Of course, after all that, I would push for a six-figure job and then—the crown of it all—get married and have kids. "After all," those in my circle would say, "if you are educated and have a good job, what else are you waiting for?" This may not have been everyone's reality, but for the

environment I grew up in, those were the expectations. I
believed that, somehow, I had to meet them all.

Saying No to the High School Boyfriend

This is beginning to sound too serious, so how about I take
you through my first encounter with romance?

I had many friends and acquaintances in high school. My
playful and outgoing nature made it easy to get along with pretty
much everyone, especially the boys. Often, the guys who I
thought were just my friends would express wanting to date me.
This would completely throw me, and I would shut their
advances down.

To give you a clearer picture of how old I was at this time, I
should point out that in Nigeria, high school is called secondary
school and is divided into two sections: Junior Secondary School
(JSS), with levels one through three, and Senior Secondary
School (SS), with levels one through three. We were admitted
into JSS1 at age nine or ten and graduated SS3 at age fifteen or
sixteen.

As a teenager, I felt I needed to understand what
relationships were about before getting into one. When I was in
JSS2, Deolu became the first guy who ever asked me to be his
girlfriend.

I asked, "What does it mean to be your girlfriend? If I say
yes, what would be next?"

Deolu had never gotten such a response, and I felt a bit silly.
He was really sought after in our school, and here I was, asking
twenty-one questions. Deep down, I knew that, at our age, it
could involve nothing more than the physical, strolling the
hallways as a couple, or exchanging gifts.

His laugh and vague response confirmed my suspicion, so my
answer was no. We remained close friends, and he dated other
girls in school.

I strongly believe that the Holy Spirit often prompted me

even when I did not know he did such things in our lives or have a full understanding of him. There was always a greater force that guided and guarded me, although I could not explain it. Regardless of how most people in high school followed the norm and had a partner, I wasn't interested in or pressured into dating anyone. This was not because I was a saint or thought dating was horrible. Besides being way too young to make boyfriends a priority, I sensed something holding me back or making me have second thoughts any time I considered dating.

My First True Love: A new relationship journey, but this time with Jesus!

The years flew by, and I continued to mature. I did not stop saying no to suitors, even at the Senior Secondary level. I had concluded that what I needed in high school was not a boyfriend or a feeling of guilt for having one, but to focus on school, build lifelong memories, and just have fun. Also, the thought of my mom offering me to my maker as what I would call a "living sacrifice" was a good enough reason to not want a boyfriend.

One Sunday morning—January 9, 2005, to be precise—someone approached me and, somehow unexplainable, I found this one person irresistible. It was a different feeling, and I had a strong conviction in my spirit that this was just the relationship I needed. At that time, I was in SS2 and had recently turned fifteen.

I was lying in bed with my grandparents that morning, and the radio was on, as usual. The only difference was, the topic being discussed caught my attention. A "prophet" was being interviewed, and he talked about a vision he'd had, claiming that there would be many ghastly accidents and plane crashes. He urged everyone listening to begin praying for Nigeria—which, as I stated earlier, is the country I grew up in and lived in at the time. He advised that each person should pray for the salvation of his or her soul and said it was by accepting Jesus as Lord and savior that every listener could be saved.

While I was at church later that Sunday,. I could not stop having conversations in my mind and asking myself, "Could this be true? Am I one of those people who need the salvation the prophet talked about? Am I really saved?"

Later that evening, I listened to another radio broadcast. This time, a lady was being interviewed, and she claimed to be God and that she made all things. She said she was omnipresent all over the world and took on different images depending on which continent she was visiting. It was the most absurd thing I had ever heard. Since I'd grown up in a Christian household, I knew something was not right with what this lady was saying. I began to feel an unrest in my spirit. I couldn't express what I was experiencing and didn't think my grandparents would understand, so I kept it to myself.

I realize now that this was the Holy Spirit guiding me to salvation. I could barely sleep that night. I just kept thinking, *I need to surrender my life to Christ. The end is drawing near.* I was not in fear of heaven or hell, but I began to question where I would spend eternity if Christ returned in that moment. I continued to ponder on the fact that I needed salvation and could only get it through Christ.

When I went back to school on Monday, I shared what I had experienced with a couple of friends, and we decided we would attend the Bible Society meeting later that week. At that meeting, I stepped out and publicly accepted Jesus as my Lord and savior, I was prayed for, and I felt so light and free. It was as though I had been carrying a heavy burden, and it was suddenly lifted. A few people gathered outside the classroom where the meeting was held and were astonished that I was there and also that I had given my life to Christ.

From that day, I began a new walk with God, and he truly was guiding and teaching me. I started to study the Bible and began to find it interesting and enjoyable to read. This was the same book I used to find boring and difficult to understand. I got a daily devotional as well and spent a lot of time studying God's word.

As time went on, I shared my encounter with as many people as I could reach in school and would encourage people to accept the invitation of salvation. I loved the joy, peace, and liberation I felt, and I wanted everyone to experience it.

Lastly, I cultivated the habit of praying and interceding for others. A few people mocked me, and I would spend time praying for them, that the Lord would speak to their hearts just as he spoke to mine. I was on a fantastic ride with Christ, and it is still the best relationship experience I have ever had in my life.

Of course, there have been times when I've felt disconnected or fallen off-track in my walk with God, but as I've grown in my faith, I have come to realize the difference between being religious—just going to church or reading my Bible as a religious act—and having a structured prayer life. I would often feel guilty if I didn't do my devotions or pray, or if I fell back into a habit I had done away with. Afterward, I would conclude that God was punishing me if anything not-so-positive happened to me. For example, when I got into an accident or didn't pass an exam, the enemy made me feel I was being punished by God for falling out of the "cycle."

I thank God for new revelation and the understanding that he is not in the business of punishing his children. His love for us is unconditional. Our talks, walk, and relationship with God do not need to take place at a specific time, in a specific place, or in a specific posture.

Who shall separate us from the love of Christ? shall tribulation, or distress, or persecution, or famine, or nakedness, or peril, or sword?

As it is written, For thy sake we are killed all the day long; we are accounted as sheep for the slaughter.

Nay, in all these things we are more than conquerors through him that loved us.

For I am persuaded, that neither death, nor life, nor angels, nor principalities, nor powers, nor things present, nor things to come,

Nor height, nor depth, nor any other creature, shall be able to separate us from the love of God, which is in Christ Jesus our Lord.

— ROMANS 8:35-39 (KJV)

The steadfast love of the Lord never ceases;
  his mercies never come to an end;
  they are new every morning;
  great is your faithfulness.

— LAMENTATIONS 3:22-23 (ESV)

When we are in Christ, we are made new, we are refined, and we are free from being conformed to the world or seeing and doing things the way the world does. Our relationship with him should be the most enjoyable one, inspiring us to remain in close and constant communication with him. Our talks with him could be just in our hearts, on our car rides or walks, as we prepare our meals, or literally at any given time, not necessarily in a specific place, at a specific time with our eyes shut, on our knees, or screaming at the top of our lungs. God has set us free from religion. He has made the ultimate sacrifice for us, and in him, we are free indeed.

I am not a perfect saint. In fact, I am far from being one. I am a work in progress, committed to daily becoming a better version of myself. I am enjoying my walk and relationship with God and striving, every day, to be more like Christ in all I do. This is, by far, my best relationship. I have found true, undiluted, and unconditional love in Christ, and I am thankful that he found me, called me his own, and loved me first.

Reflection and Prayer

Think back to the day you met Christ and dedicated your life to him. Thank him for making the ultimate sacrifice for you and for his unending love for you.

CHAPTER 2

THE BACKGROUND NOISE

Now that I better understood real love, which is Christ's love for me, I set the bar even higher when it came to the kind of person I would marry. I knew how deep God's love was for me, and the beautiful picture of marriage he painted in the scriptures was what I desired to have.

Instructions for Christian Households

Submit to one another out of reverence for Christ.

Wives, submit yourselves to your own husbands as you do to the Lord. For the husband is the head of the wife as Christ is the head of the church, his body, of which he is the Savior. Now as the church submits to Christ, so also wives should submit to their husbands in everything.

Husbands, love your wives, just as Christ loved the church and gave himself up for her to make her holy, cleansing her by the washing with water through the word, and to present her to himself as a radiant church, without stain or wrinkle or any other blemish, but holy and blameless. In this same way, husbands ought to love their wives as their own bodies. He who loves his wife loves himself. After all, no one ever hated their own body, but they feed and care for their body, just as Christ does the church—for we are members of his body. "For this reason

a man will leave his father and mother and be united to his wife, and
the two will become one flesh." This is a profound mystery—but I am
talking about Christ and the church. However, each one of you also must
love his wife as he loves himself, and the wife must respect her husband.

— EPHESIANS 5:22-33 (NIV)

The Relationships I Witnessed

Since I have always been passionate about the institution of marriage, I did a lot of deep thinking and soul searching on the topic. Over the years, I watched those around me, listened to speakers, and read a great deal about marriage. The relationships I witnessed were nothing like those described in the Bible, or even the marriages portrayed on TV and in movies. I mostly saw divorce, separation, and toxic or abusive relationships—the complete opposite of the beautiful picture of marriage painted in Ephesians 5: 22-33.

TV shows and movies often depict marriage as a perfect happy ending. Your Prince Charming finds you, and after a beautiful wedding, you have fantastic lives from then on. However, the marriages I saw in reality, even in my own family, were not encouraging. I watched people lose themselves, alter their destinies, and forgo their purposes because of marriage. I saw first-hand how married people were used and abused. Somehow, I was supposed to accept the infidelity, verbal and emotional abuse, disrespect, hostility, and toxicity I witnessed as normal, but this was *not* what a Godly marriage should look like.

First Generation: My Grandma

I was raised by a single mom and my grandparents. Mom was divorced, but my grandparents were married for over fifty years before my grandfather passed away. My grandmother literally served my grandfather every day. Her mornings often started with making him tea and breakfast before she began her devotions. She prepared all his meals on demand and, when she would be out at church or attending an event, she constantly watched the clock so she could get back home in time to prepare her husband's next meal. She did this every day until he died. She shared stories of how he had children with other women and how she'd endured pain, suffering, spiritual attacks, and all sorts of negativity in her marriage.

She was taught that she had to hang in there because of her children. To her, it was worth everything she'd endured, because her husband stayed with her until he passed and her children were all doing well. She claimed she was reaping the fruits of her labor, but this made me wonder why anybody would want to venture into a journey that could be so toxic and painful.

Second Generation: My Mom

I never had a full nuclear family unit, since my parents had lived apart from my earliest memory. My brother and I are seven years apart. Mom shared just a few stories about our dad, and my grandma shared some, too. Though I grew up not knowing my dad, my maternal grandfather was all the father I needed and more.

My mom worked hard to provide for our little family and give us the best. We went to some of the best schools and lacked nothing. She worked tirelessly and made many sacrifices to ensure that we were comfortable.

I was an average student in elementary and high school, so in addition to paying my school fees, my mom paid for me to attend tutorials after school. I would come home from those to a private tutor. Boy! My mom did not play when it came to our education. I attended more lessons and tutorials than social or recreational activities. She gave her best singlehandedly and by God's grace.

To this day, she has given only a vague explanation for why

my dad left her to raise two children on her own. She said he was under a spiritual attack, which caused him to develop an inexplicable hatred for his wife. I wish I knew more, but that's the story I was told, and I guess that's what we're sticking with!

A little over twenty years after my parents' divorce, the spiritual attack expired, and my dad found his way back to Mom. I was about twenty-three and mostly independent, and this was one reunion I did not understand or see coming. I'd never even imagined that I would ever meet my dad.

My mom, her brothers, and even my dad himself expected me to accept this stranger and live happily ever after. However, those were some of the worst moments of my life to that point. My mom and I had the worst arguments ever, and that was even more hurtful because it was over a person with whom I had no emotional connection. How was I supposed to have a "kumbaya" relationship with a father who had just reappeared?

Mom and my uncles kept saying that I needed to forgive my dad and let go. I didn't understand that either, because I'd never felt he offended me or did wrong to me. What did I need to forgive him for? I hadn't suffered or lacked anything. Aside from the way he'd wronged my mom, I didn't blame him for anything. My mom was able to instantly forgive him, and I applaud her for that, but I could not accept him infusing himself into my life and dictating what I should or shouldn't do, instantly playing the role of a father when he knew nothing about me.

But to focus on marriage, my mom's reconnection with her husband after so many years brought her great joy. She was like a teenager, having a crush all over again. She would text her friends and spend hours on the phone, telling them she was back with her long-lost husband. She got another chance at happiness, and God incredibly repaid her for all the years of pain and being alone. It really was a miracle and testimony, because it's almost unheard of. A romantic reconnection after a separation of over twenty years—and neither of them had married other people?

Eventually, my dad and I formed a cordial relationship and

spoke from time to time. Unfortunately, he passed away about three years after his fairytale reunion with Mom. But he left a spark in her life that remains.

My Circle: Mimi

My friend Mimi, who has become like a sister, was in a marriage filled with pain. Her then-husband was emotionally abusive, cheated on her, lied to her, and stole from her. This hell-on-Earth experience almost cost her life. As she watched her whole life shatter, she blamed herself for allowing it to happen.

She once told me, "A knife pierced through my heart, but I let that knife in there."

As she later reflected on this devastating situation, she could attribute some of her decisions to pressure. She'd heard it all—that she was not getting any younger; that all men are the same, they cheat; and that she had to hang in there. But she could only hang for so long. The marriage lasted only a few months.

Hallelujah!! Mimi got another chance to love, but this time, not on anybody else's clock. Biology didn't even have a say. Only God did. She decided to wait and completely depend on God for his choice of a spouse for her. She did her time, though it was difficult, some days, to hang on and keep the faith. She persevered, and eventually the wait paid.

Her God-ordained husband found her in a place and at a time she did not expect. He gave her beauty for ashes. I can testify to how beautifully God rescripted her story and blessed her with a biblical marriage. She calls him "the God of not just one, two, or three chances, but the God of many chances."

My Circle: Esther

Another friend of mine married the boyfriend of her youth. She was nineteen when their relationship began. After they both finished school and were working, marriage was next on the list.

That was the order and pattern our society had drawn up for us, and my dear friend, whom I will call Esther, was right on track.

Her marriage was blessed with a wonderful son. Since she had this child, she felt she had to endure her husband's infidelity and physical, verbal, and emotional abuse. She spent a lot of time fighting and praying for the marriage to work. Since she invested all her time and energy in the situation, she couldn't see the possibility of reaching her dreams. When she cried out for help, she, too, was advised to hang in there and to stay for her son. People gave her such unhelpful advice as, "The grass is not greener on the other side," blah-blah-blah.

In her words, "I didn't know then what I know now. I got married because I thought it was the right thing to do. I was told to hang in there, so I did, till I couldn't, anymore. I went to God, this time."

Esther's story is another testimony of God's mercy and how he gives his children another chance. God gave her the courage and direction to step out of the situation. He brought her out of the horrible pit and set her feet upon an unshakable rock. God transformed her life, and she broke barriers in her career. I proudly call her my doctor friend, as she furthered her education to a doctorate level in nursing, started her own businesses, and owns her own home.

My Waiting Game

Without being married, I got to see a lot of the highs and lows of marriage and was determined that I must get it right. I had to marry God's way and by God's choice. I couldn't afford to make a mistake in that aspect of my life. I had seen too much and often would say, "I can live with failing in other areas but not marriage." So, if I had to wait, however long it took, I was ready to wait. I understood that the fulfillment of my purpose and my destiny was tied to whoever I married. I couldn't play games there!

As you may have figured out by now, the story and aspect of my life that birthed this book is really my period of waiting for the gift and blessing of marriage.

I had so much faith and a clear image of how beautifully things would turn out for me. My peers who were already married didn't make me feel pressured. It was their time and not mine. I was comfortable being a third wheel with friends and their partners and got used to being the single girl at the table during events. My man and my time would come. However, other situations bothered me.

Despite all I knew about God's timing and promises, I had moments when I would break down and ask that daunting question: "God, why me?" Or rather, why *not* me? Then, I'd make my case to God. "I've kept myself pure. I've served in your house. I pray, fast, and give. I bless weddings, trying my best to be kind and genuinely love and celebrate others. God, why am I not able to connect with anyone?"

Those were the toughest, most painful moments of my wait. Regardless of how clearly I knew that God had great plans for me, there were still many nights when I cried myself to sleep, wondering why. Especially since I felt I was ready. I sometimes found myself almost wanting to pull my hair out, full of frustration and feeling unwanted, at least by the kind of man I desired and prayed for. Even though I was used to being single, certain events truly made me feel lonely. I would wonder, for instance, why I was attending this Valentine's Ball, single. Why was I at this wedding without a date? Why was I the only one at this birthday dinner without a partner?

Social Media didn't help matters. I would see posts from girls much younger than I was who were getting engaged or married. I would send congratulations to the girl but ask, "Lord, where have I gone wrong?"

God's answer? "Why not you?" He would repeatedly remind me that he had a purpose for my life, I had a story, and he had to be ascribed all of the glory. He wanted to prove through my life and my story that he is God, and that he can do exceedingly, abundantly, above all I could ask or think. He even reminded me of the story of Lazarus to make his point.

Lazarus had died, and his sisters believed he would have still been alive if Jesus had arrived sooner.

When Jesus heard about this, he said, "Lazarus's sickness will not end in death. No, it happened for the glory of God so that the Son of God will receive glory from this" (John 11:4 NLT).

The story of Lazarus may sound extreme, but I could relate it to my situation. My delay, my singleness, my *wait* was not going to end in sadness. It had to be this way so the son of God would receive all the glory, just like he did when Lazarus was raised from death. Though I knew all this and the profound truth of it filled my spirit, the background noise would still make me ask God, "Why me?"

Friends would ask, "Yimi, what's going on? Any guy or guys in the picture? Are you being too picky?"

Year in and year out, I would give the same, almost cliché, responses. "There is no one yet," or "God's time is the best," or "It will happen very soon." It really was frustrating.

Aunties at church would pull me to the side and advise me not to set my standards too high in my choice of partner. They cautioned me not to look down on anyone. On a few occasions, people tried to hook me up with their nephews or brothers or cousins in different parts of the world. I was even advised to tone down my makeup, not dress too flashy, and stop wearing my gold rings, since these things could deter potential suitors from approaching me.

One very dear church aunty introduced me to her nephew in the UK. He seemed like a great guy, but we just didn't connect. I tried to be more open to the idea, just so I wouldn't disappoint or offend my aunty, but it didn't work out.

The same aunty later encouraged me to try online dating. I was hesitant because I never felt convicted to go that path. Don't get me wrong, I am not against online dating. It has worked for some people. In fact, Godly relationships and marriages have stemmed from online dating. I just wasn't led to do it. Aunty gave me examples of people it had worked for, trying to persuade me to give it a shot, so I agreed.

I picked up my laptop that evening and typed in a dating site's address. The first page prompted me to create a profile. I fixed my eyes on the screen, and my fingers were glued to my keyboard, but they grew numb. I sat there as if in a movie that had been paused, no words appearing on my screen. I forced my fingers down to begin typing a username, and suddenly, a loud and clear voice spoke in my heart, saying this was not my path. I grabbed my phone and sent a text to Aunty, explaining what had happened and letting her know God had not released me to try online dating. She was very understanding and continued to wish me well.

I listened to every piece of advice with gratitude, knowing it came from a place of care and love. Still, deep down, I would ask God, "But why?"

I didn't understand why people felt the need to mount so much pressure. I was living in the US and in my mid to late twenties by then, a few years past the age when I'd hoped to be married. I had adjusted to waiting on God's time, and this minimized the feelings of any time constraint or the age pressure I'd placed on myself. I guess some people assumed I was much older, since I have a circle of friends who are older than I am.

Whatever their reasons, the only prayer anyone seemed to offer for me involved marriage. I hardly heard anyone pray for me to prosper and be in good health, or that I would continue to excel in my career. Instead, people would say, "You will marry soon," "It will soon be your turn," or "God will bless you with a good husband." All I needed, after all, was a husband.

One Saturday morning, my grandma called me from Nigeria. It was so early, I was barely awake. When I asked if everything was okay, she said that she needed to talk to me and wanted my full attention. My heart raced because I was clueless where she was going with the conversation. Then, she asked how old I was.

"Twenty-seven," I said.

"You are no longer a child and should be married," she said. "All your friends from church and high school are married, and some have children. So, what, exactly, are you waiting for?"

Then, she advised me not to be picky or wait for a man who was already "made." I'm not sure why she thought I was waiting for a readymade man, but she said I should be open to starting and growing with a man.

"It breaks my heart that you are not married, and I see how it breaks your mom's, too." She started to cry and begged me to get married.

I was numb, confused, shocked, cold, and sad all at the same time. After she hung up, I cried, "God, why?"

As I got older, these pressures made me feel insecure about myself. Maybe I was the problem, and I was the reason why the few counterfeit relationships I'd had (which I will share with you in the next chapter) didn't work. Perhaps it wasn't that I was picky, but that I was just not brilliant enough. Or I must be unattractive. Maybe it was my flat bum, or my lumpy nose, or my big arms, or my dark skin. Perhaps I needed to wear more makeup, more name-brand clothes, or extensions. I mean, I had prayed and prayed, fasted, praised, cried, complained...you name it. Regardless of the truth I knew about God's thoughts and plans for me, how clearly I knew what I wanted in a husband, or how deeply I wanted to do relationships God's way at all costs, the pressures of this world made me feel unworthy and that I was the cause of my own delay.

Through the highs and lows of this waiting game, it was evident that God's hand was upon my life. Even when I was down, lonely, or asking why, I just could not stay there. I couldn't wallow in sorrow, doubt, or self-pity. It was never long before I wiped my tears and moved on, because God always reminded me of my purpose.

Reflection and Prayer

What are some areas in which you have felt pressured by the people or circumstances around you? Thank God for the grace to overcome any pressures of the world. Commit all of those pressures to God and thank him for lifting every burden.

CHAPTER 3

MY WILL VERSUS GOD'S WILL

Although I was determined to be careful in making relationship decisions, not just dating for fun, I was also praying to meet the right person. Over the years, I met a few guys who, I thought, could be the answer to my prayers. One thing I realized is that the more fervently you pray about something, the more you'll start to encounter options that look or feel like the answer, and you begin to wonder if those are signs from God. It's like developing interest in a certain car. The moment you go to the dealership to test drive the car, it seems like all the roads are suddenly filled with the exact same car or something similar. In reality, you just notice them a lot more.

Imitation Gold

Shortly after I moved to the US to attend college when I was sixteen, I experienced my first real crush. I'd actually met Dan while visiting my relatives in America on a summer holiday, but he'd shown no interest in me. He was a close friend of my cousin, so when I moved in with my relatives to attend college, I saw him often. Our families were also acquainted, which created more opportunities for us to be around each other.

One day, my cousin mentioned that Dan was sick and in the hospital. I was so worried and prayed he would recover soon. Eventually, I summoned the courage to call him to see how he was doing, but he didn't pick up. I left a message, saying I was just checking in, and wished him a speedy recovery. About two days later, on a Friday night, my phone rang, and it was him. My heart skipped. I couldn't believe Dan was calling me. I finally picked up. Though I have no recollection of what we talked about, one hour became two, and two became three. I ended up sitting in a closet in the basement so I wouldn't disturb the rest of the house with my giggling and laughing all night.

This call was the beginning of a very interesting friendship. Dan and I spoke every day and every night. His family and mine attended the same church, and we would look forward to meeting up there. He often came over with my cousin and other friends to spend time with us after church. Sometimes, he even asked what I would be wearing for church, so he could color-coordinate with me.

Dan was older than me, so a bit more settled in his career, and came from a good, close-knit, Christian family. He was very comfortable taking me to family and social functions, and boy, his sisters loved me! They adopted me from the get-go and called me their little sister. I had a great relationship with his family, and his sisters would tease him about cradle-snatching me, as I was not quite eighteen. They would mention on occasion that they would love to have me as their sister in-law.

Everything seemed perfect. We never argued, and we spoke about everything. At least, that was what I believed. He was a Christian, generally a nice person, and seemed to be very into me. After all, he gave me a lot of attention, more attention than I had ever received from a guy. I thought God had answered my prayers, and I was thankful that he had while I was so young, since I wouldn't have to keep searching. This had to be it. I just had to wait for the official ask or commitment.

We got so intertwined in each other's lives, we knew the

details of each other's schedules. As soon as I would step out of class, he would call. Sometimes, he picked me up from school and gave me a ride home. He told me often that he enjoyed talking to me and felt I was so mature, especially for my age. We never gave this friendship a label, but it felt like we were dating, considering how much time we spent together in person or over the phone.

Many nights, we both fell asleep talking on the phone. Once, when he was sick and in the hospital, I borrowed my uncle's car in the rain to take him lunch and spend time with him. I had just started driving and didn't have my own car yet. On the nights when he couldn't sleep, I would stay up on the phone all night to keep him company, then get up in the morning to get ready for class.

This friendship went on for close to a year, and I began to sense him withdrawing. He mentioned that his ex-girlfriend was celebrating her twenty-fifth birthday and he planned to attend. Everything went downhill from there, as he barely contacted me. I have never been one to call people profusely, except if there's an emergency, so I called once. He didn't call back for days, which was very unlike him.

I consoled myself with the fact that Dan had never officially asked me to be his girlfriend or made any commitments to me. This meant I was not at all entitled to him.

Though my memory of this is vague, I believe things didn't go very smoothly with his ex, so he came back around. Of course, I was open to continuing the friendship. We became just as close as we were before his detour. Months went by, and Dan enrolled in some post-graduate classes in his previous university, which required him to stay out there a few nights each week. He decided to stay with another university ex-girlfriend, and the cycle started again. I wouldn't hear from him at all when he was gone. It finally dawned on me that he was just stringing me along, since I happened to always be available. Back then, I was very timid and didn't ask many commitment-related questions, so I wouldn't come off as needy or desperate.

By this time, I had matured a lot and was more aware of what I wanted in a relationship. This inconsistency and lack of commitment couldn't have been God's will for my life. It was my very first attempt at being in a committed relationship, but the commitment was lacking on his part. I summoned the courage and asked Dan where this "friendship" was headed and whether there was a reason we hadn't made a commitment.

He said I was a great girl and would make a perfect wife, and any man would be lucky to have me. However, he loved the friendship we had and wouldn't want anything to ruin it, so he wanted us to just continue getting to know each other.

I asked the same question on a different occasion, and he responded with some proverb about not wanting to make his wife a girlfriend.

That left me with the impression that I could be his wife, so there was no need for me to even want the girlfriend title. Of course, this sounded fine to me. I had no need to pressure him into a commitment. Things seemed to go okay for a while until someone told me Dan might be talking to another girl who lived out of state. Again, I was not sure whether to confront him, as I didn't feel I had any right to do so. Then, after he had begun to get comfortable again when we hung out with friends on Sundays, he got carried away one afternoon and mentioned this girl he was checking out on Facebook.

Some days, I felt sad because I had grown so fond of Dan and enjoyed spending time with him. I had become part of his family and truly thought he would be my husband. I felt that he had taken advantage of my naïveté and I hadn't been brave enough to let go. As I found myself in this state of confusion and mixed emotions, I decided to talk to the one person who has never let me down.

I started to pray a lot more about Dan, asking God for clarity and direction. I realized I had been caught up in the moment and never sought God's face on where this relationship was supposed to be heading. A sudden thought struck me, that I had not asked God to make things work out or help me win Dan's heart. That told me all I needed to know.

I then prayed fervently for the willpower to cut every emotional tie and move forward, unhurt, from the friendship. I asked for grace to desire absolutely nothing from Dan from then on. I prayed for the grace and strength to deal with our romantic friendship ending, because I began to see the end of it. Although this was disappointing, I had never experienced a heartbreak and did *not* want to do so now.

I had prayed very early in life for a husband, and Dan had perfectly fit the criteria of what I desired. Since I'd had a crush on him first, what were the odds that he would be interested in me? It was all false, though. An imitation, a knock-off, a lookalike of what I truly desired from God. It couldn't have been the real deal, because God's will is definite. It is consistent, not confused or uncertain. Thankfully, the scales had fallen off my eyes. This was another indication of how precious I was to God, and how he always has looked out for me and always will.

Soon after this, Dan called me out of the blue, after he had gone three days without contacting me. I told him, flat out, not to call me anymore.

When he asked why, I said, "No reason. I just don't want you to call me any longer."

He said, "Okay, if that's what you want."

Strangely, it felt like I had been delivered from bondage that day. I felt lighter, as though I had carried a burden and it was suddenly lifted. The very day I had the courage to end the entanglement, my heart rested at total peace for the first time in almost two years. That was it for me. Regardless of what Dan's intentions might be, I was delivered completely.

On the occasions when he would try to be nice to me, ask me to be his date to a wedding, or offer to buy me things, my answer remained *no*. Somehow, turning him down did not hurt, and I knew without a doubt that this was God at work.

Since Dan and I were family friends, went to the same church, and were in the same social circle, our paths still crossed. We were able to maintain a cordial friendship with mutual respect and no lingering feelings of attachment. I experienced not an iota of pain or regret. More than anything, I was thankful to God and had even higher expectations of what the future held for me.

As time went by, I discovered that the rumors were true, and Dan had been talking with a lady in another state. She came around often and was friendly with everyone in Dan's circle. She relocated to Minnesota, and we eventually became close friends —almost inseparable, in fact. With great joy, I celebrated many milestones with them. It was a pleasure to watch their love blossom into marriage and a wonderful family.

When I had the opportunity—before they were married, of course—I did ask Dan, just for clarity and closure, what exactly happened with our relationship.

He said, "I just wasn't serious."

His answer somehow sufficed, and it was satisfying to know that there was nothing wrong on my end. God had just preserved me for my real and timeless piece of gold.

A Total Knock-Off

A few years after my relationship with Dan ended, his wife— we'll call her Sonia—and I remained good friends. On a trip to Chicago with her, I met some of her friends. One of them was Femi. He seemed pleasant, and we had a few things in common career-wise, which made conversing with him easy. He was in a relationship, so I had absolutely no expectation of dating him. We stayed in touch here and there, and I asked about his degree program since I was looking to get into the same one.

While I was studying in the UK for my master's program—

which I discuss in more detail in another chapter—Femi would check in from time to time, to see how I was doing and how school was going. One day, he also asked if I would be attending Dan and Sonia's wedding, as he was hoping to see me. I thought that was very kind of him, but my final exams were scheduled around the time of their wedding, so I wasn't able to attend.

Once I wrapped up my program and returned to the States, Femi and I kept in contact a bit more frequently. He followed up on the progress of my dissertation. I think I may have shared a draft of it with him to get his thoughts on it. He was super excited for me when I finished, and we were able to chat more, mainly on WhatsApp, which is an instant messenger application. In one of our conversations, he told me he was no longer in a relationship, and I thought that explained why he kept in touch a bit more frequently.

We became closer friends and got to know each other a bit more, all via chat. He had told me he was not big on talking on the phone but was okay chatting. This disturbed me a little. I mean, if I'm trying to get to know someone, I would at least want to actually talk to him. Still, I did not make an issue of it.

He made a lot of effort to ask personal questions—about my views on marriage, my walk with God, ministry, and even my comfort level with relocating or changing churches. Based on the questions he asked, I assumed he might be considering a relationship with me. We stayed in contact like this for a few months, speaking very seldom but chatting every so often. We sometimes teased each other about one of us missing the other. In one of those moments, I asked when he would come visit.

He said that he could come visit but wondered where he would stay. He felt he couldn't stay with his friend Sonia, since she was now married.

I told him he could stay with me, as I was in the process of moving. My brother was also living in the US, and he and I had decided to move into a townhouse together. I was going to have the house to myself for a few months before he came to join me, so there was more than enough space. The thought of Femi coming to visit thrilled me, since I'd finally get a chance to talk to him in person and get clarity on where our chats were headed. I also prayed that, if God had any plans for us to be together, this would be revealed during Femi's visit. We had been chatting for a while, and I was anxious to know what the future held.

I looked forward to this visit until about two months later, when Sonia informed me of her plans to hold a thirtieth birthday party for Dan. Coincidentally, it fell on the same weekend Femi had suggested coming to visit me. She had invited him and a few other friends from Chicago, and Femi figured he could probably stay with me. Once I discovered all of this, I was a little disappointed, but I thought it would be unfair to say he was not welcome anymore.

As the event drew closer, I asked Femi if he would let Sonia know he planned to stay at my house or if I needed to discuss it with her as a courtesy. I had never been in such a situation and wasn't sure what the protocols were on accommodating a friend-of-a-friend who had now also become my friend. He told me he'd mentioned to her that I would be picking him up from the airport, but he would also inform her of his plans to stay with me.

A few weeks later, Sonia and I were discussing some of the plans for the birthday party and sharing some estimates she had gotten from the caterer. All was dandy till later that afternoon, when I got another message from her.

"So, Femi is staying with you, and you're picking him up?" she asked. "He said you offered to host him."

I told her I had, since he said he wasn't sure he could stay with her. I had two spare rooms, so I didn't mind hosting him or the rest of his friends.

The remainder of that conversion did not go smoothly at all. Sonia said I had no right to host her guest. I was out of pocket to have said that someone she brought around me was my friend.

If he and I wanted to meet up, it should not be on her invitation, but at a different time.

I was in total shock. How could my friend, who was married, have such a big problem with my hosting a guy who I truly thought had become a mutual friend. "Address it with Femi," I said. "He is an adult and can determine what he wants to do or where he wants to stay."

"I did address it with him," she said, "and he apologized, and here you are, being defensive as though he is your man. You were out of line, and you will never understand."

She ended the conversation abruptly, and nothing I said mattered. She was right, I would never understand. Even now, many years later, I still don't. I felt so hurt and disrespected. The situation was even more painful because I got such a backlash from a friend who knew I was hoping and praying to be in a relationship at the time.

Many thoughts ran through my mind. I believed this was God's way of withdrawing any feelings I may have been developing for Femi, because it seemed I would owe the relationship to Sonia and might always have to seek permission for anything I did that pertained to Femi. I also became more wary of Femi. Could I trust him? He'd given me the impression that he wanted to come visit *me*; however, all along he'd had a birthday party to attend.

First, I asked God that, at all costs, when it was time for me to meet my husband, it would not be a hookup or an introduction made by someone else. My husband himself would find me and desire me. I was determined that no man would get an ounce of glory in my husband finding me. All the glory would be ascribed to God.

Secondly, I decided I would respect whatever decision Femi made on where he wanted to stay. If he did decide to stay with me, I would be a courteous host, and that would be it.

Sonia didn't speak to me for over a week, until I reached out to her to request that we meet and address the issue. I made peace with her, and we moved on. Femi did decide to stay with me as planned, but he gave me no explanations for what had transpired with Sonia, and I let it be.

After I picked him up, Femi and I had lunch and went out later for dessert. We spent most of the time talking about everything but us. By evening, we ran out of things to talk about —or perhaps neither of us was bold enough to say what was truly on our minds. I asked my friend Mimi to come over, just to ease some of the awkwardness between Femi and me as we got ready for the party.

After we arrived at the party, Femi hung out with his friends. I spent time with mine and enjoyed the night. Once it was over and we went home, we barely spoke. We knew we would only get a couple hours of sleep, because Femi and his friends had a very early flight to catch. When morning came, we went to pick up his friends at their hotel, I dropped them off at the airport, and that was goodbye.

Clearly, God had given me no go-ahead on this matter. Femi was not one to really communicate, and befriending him was already causing a rift between me and a supposed close friend. Somehow, though, I still had a little ounce of hope that something could work out.

Femi didn't stop contacting me, even though the conversations lacked substance in every sense. We chatted almost every other day about nothing, really, but I kept hoping one day he would come out with his feelings. I was not going to bring it up. This continued for another three months, which brought us to the end of the year.

One day, in the first week of the new year, Femi texted, teasing and asking about my boyfriend. I had learned the spiritual principle of speaking about what we want as though it has already become a reality—speaking in faith. So, I responded, by faith, as though I really was seeing someone. I told Femi I was courting a guy, and his name was Iremide. This name, which means "my goodness has come," was what I called my future husband when praying about him. We chatted some more, and Femi said he was happy for me, although he had thought I was "the one." Now that I was seeing someone, he said, he figured he must have been wrong.

I couldn't believe what I was reading. It had to be a joke! After almost a year of talking about nothing, he suddenly says he thought I was the one? I decided he had to be kidding and that I didn't need to tell him I wasn't actually seeing anyone.

Femi stopped checking in or chatting with me until about a month later, when I posted a photo of a friend's engagement ring as my display picture on WhatsApp. He asked if I had gotten engaged and said he would be sad if I had. I was a little confused and slightly irritated at the same time. I went on a rant about how long he and I had been talking and how much time and attention I gave him. How on Earth could he think I was truly seeing someone else, let alone engaged? I told him he was being ridiculous.

On the contrary, he said I was being ridiculous and that I had done something terrible by making him believe I was in a relationship for the past month. Everything he said continued to indicate how horrible our communication had been.

Slowly, I started to regret what I had done. Maybe my joke was a little too expensive. Just at the time when it seemed that Femi was becoming a bit more vocal with his feelings, I had pushed him farther away. I wasn't sure what to do.

He played it off like nothing major had happened, until he said, "If only you knew. I still love you, but it's too late."

At that moment, I knew I had really messed up. I spent the whole night thinking of what I could do and how I could fix it. If he really was the one for me, I didn't want to lose him over a petty joke. We kept chatting for a couple of weeks, and it didn't seem like much had changed between us. However, deep down, I kept waiting to see if he would tell me what the next steps were after this huge revelation, or if I needed to brace myself to ask directly.

Now that we seemed to both be more transparent with our feelings, I eventually summoned the courage to ask Femi where we could go from here. I'd just found out a few days before that my dad had suddenly passed away, and I hoped some level of certainty where Femi was concerned would give me comfort and a sense of stability.

Femi said he was now in a relationship with another girl and was waiting to see how things would go with her. If that did not work out and I happened to be available, he would seek God's direction on how to properly pursue me.

I couldn't believe what I had heard. I was shattered. How could he go from thinking I was the one to suddenly being with someone else? Why was I so unlucky? My heart raced and pounded. I started hyperventilating, and I didn't know how to make it stop. I wanted to brush off his words, let it go, and just feel better, but I could not make it stop. I curled up in my bed and wept bitterly till I fell asleep.

The next day, I wasn't able to function at work. I kept running out of breath. First, I'd lost my dad, whom I had just met three years before and was finally getting along with, and now this with Femi? All types of emotions ran through my mind that day. I just needed someone to talk to, so I called Sonia. She rushed down to my office that evening to comfort me and pointed out that what I was feeling was a heartbreak, but that I was going to be okay.

Fortunately, a church conference kicked off that night. At this aptly-named Solution Conference, I found the ultimate comfort. Being in God's presence started the healing process, and I felt better as the days passed.

You may get a kick out of how I had gotten myself into yet another weird entanglement. Apparently, Femi had met his current girl at Dan's wedding. She was Dan's cousin! I could hardly believe it when he told me, but I was thankful that, once again, the Lord had looked out for me.

Femi and I did remain good friends, because I understood

that he was not meant for me, and I accepted that with all my heart. Many months later, he was courteous enough to inform me of his intentions to propose to his girlfriend. He said he didn't want me to be caught unawares. I appreciated that and genuinely wished him well.

Truthfully, I thought I was okay until I saw pictures and videos of the engagement. I couldn't hold the tears back and was inconsolable. My brother did all he could to cheer me up, but I couldn't stop crying. By this time, I had learned and grown, was at peace, and had concluded that Femi was a total knock-off for my intended husband. He definitely was not the real gold God had in store for me. Still, I cried bitterly, not because I was unhappy about Femi's engagement. Deep down, I knew he wasn't the one I had been praying for all these years, but I couldn't bear to start my wait for a husband again. That made me feel defeated.

Femi might have initially seemed like a good potential husband, but God wouldn't want me to be with someone I couldn't talk to freely. He also wouldn't want me to be with someone who lacked clear direction, nor would he want me to be anyone's Plan B or second choice. He loves me so much more than that. I am his beloved, the apple of his eye, to be desired, loved, wanted, needed, found, and cherished. I had discovered my worth and was even more determined to completely depend on God to choose a partner for me.

I made an agreement with God that when he was ready to bless me with my husband, the man had to be the one to find me, desire me, and pursue me. I would have complete peace. My intended husband would not be confused, and neither would I, because God is never an author of confusion.

Reflection and Prayer

There may be some things you have wanted at all costs. It could be a relationship that did not work out or a job opportunity you lost. Thank God, now, for lost opportunities and for shielding you from an imitation of his real plans for your life.

CHAPTER 4

MY WAIT-TIME PRAYERS

Neither my failed relationships nor the things I had seen others experience could deter me from desiring marriage. Although I had missed the timeline I set for myself and was well over twenty-five years old now, I was still certain marriage was part of God's plan for my life and an avenue toward fulfilling my purpose. I had not escaped the unfruitful relationships to remain unmarried forever, God had a better plan. With that understanding, I intentionally prepared for marriage. I already had a deep love for anything that related to weddings—and marriage, in general.

My Obsession with Weddings

Oh, my goodness! I lived for weddings. I loved anything wedding-related. I watched almost every wedding video on YouTube, just for fun. Some, I watched more than once, as if they were classic movies. At times, I would cry through a video, either in admiration of the beauty and love it showed, or because I was wondering when it would be my turn.

Weddings were one event I had a flare for. I went through the wedding preparation process with many brides, scheduling dress trials for some, planning a number of bridal showers, picking wedding bouquets, handcrafting wedding invites and programs, going cake tasting or "saying yes to the dress" with brides. During the "make it rain" portion of the wedding reception, I was the girl who would be on her hands and knees packing up the dollar bills raining on the dancing couple. I did everything possible to ensure that my friends who were brides had all they needed.

I have been a bridesmaid about fifteen times and travelled as far as Nigeria, London, and Malta for my bridesmaids' duties. I've served as both an in-person bridesmaid and a virtual one. I've been an add-on bridesmaid for friends and acquaintances. You name it! It really was a lot of fun—expensive fun. It didn't matter who it was or where it was, if it was a wedding, I was all in, baby!

I am sharing this somewhat silly side of me in hopes that I do not come off as weird. Since marriage was something I desired, prayed for, and saw in my future, I needed to love it every step of the way. This doesn't mean that everyone should now develop an interest in weddings or become half-obsessed as I was. Absolutely not!

For me, this was part of my preparation and my determination to do things by faith. As I watched wedding videos, I envisioned what mine would look like. As I helped my friends plan their weddings, I took notes for myself. I was sowing a seed by faith, knowing that, one day, it would be my turn. I gave generously and prayed and fasted with friends who were getting married. Regardless of what the world said about marriages being likely to end in separation or divorce, I spoke God's word over my friends' unions. I joined my faith with theirs, that their marriages would glorify God.

I believe strongly that you cannot become what you cannot see, and you cannot become what you envy. Living by these two principles, I imagined myself as a bride while I blessed others, wished them well, and prayed for them. I didn't envy or get jealous of anyone, but had an understanding that our timing was different. Instead, I was genuinely happy for others and celebrated them. There was no doubt in my heart that my turn, day, and time of celebration would come. I was waiting, preparing, and loving it!

What I Wanted in a Man: My List

Opinions differ regarding making a list of what you want in a spouse. Some people believe that doing so will confine them to a certain type of person, or that it could mean they're being too picky and looking for a perfect partner (which does not exist).

Though I understood the thinking behind those beliefs, I felt it was important that I knew exactly what I wanted—not just in a man, but in my future husband. For that reason, I needed to have a list, to write what I desired and make it plain. I believed that, if I didn't know precisely what I wanted, then I would be open to anything and anyone. So, at various points in my life, I made a list. I think I ended up with three versions of this list, and I updated it with every new understanding I gained about marriage.

My lists were very lengthy, humorous, and a bit much, to be honest. I laughed each time I read one and even ended them with the question, "Does such a man even exist?" Still, I was confident in the God I served. To mankind, my list may be ridiculous, but to God, nothing was ridiculous.

Regardless of how funny my list seemed, I knew that all I had to do was make my requests known to God. If something was important to me, then it was important to God. His word also says "Do not be anxious about anything, but in every situation, by prayer and petition, with thanksgiving, present your requests to God" (Philippians 4:6 NIV). With this word, I was able to do just that, make my "ridiculous" request known to the one who is able to do beyond what I could ask or think.

So, I made my list and prayed about it every now and then,

trusting that my desires would align with God's plan for my life. Regardless of what I had written down, it was more important to me that I would receive God's best.

Corporate Prayers

I cannot overemphasize the importance of prayer—not just while trusting God for something, but over every situation of life. The Bible tells us, "[...] if two of you on earth agree about anything they ask for, it will be done for them by my Father in heaven" (Matthew 18:19 NIV). For this reason, I prayed independently about my desire to be married. I also prayed with certain friends.

On my birthday in 2016, my friends and I decided to celebrate together and hold a night vigil. Mimi, Tope, Sayo, and I met up at Sayo's apartment. She and Tope had cooked up a storm. We ate, I cut my birthday cake, we took pictures, and had some good laughs. When our meals had digested, we started the after party—the Holy Ghost party where we expressed our appreciation of how far God had brought us. At the time, we were all trusting God for a spouse, in addition to other personal things, and we agreed together in prayer that night. We worshipped and prayed together. It was indeed a sacrifice of praise, because Mimi struggled to stay awake. Ha-ha.

The following year—I believe it was November of 2017—Mimi and I were still in our waiting process and decided to have a seven-day prayer and fasting session, specifically for our future husbands. This was another sacrifice well worth it, because about two months later, Mimi's prayer request became a praise report. Her husband found her! Praise the Lord, somebody!

I share this because, for me, it was a huge blessing to have friends who didn't just have fun together, but could come together to agree on a matter in prayer. While trusting God, it is vital that we surround ourselves with people who are equally yoked—who stand in the gap for one another, speak life and positivity over an issue, and pray together. We need to avoid or minimize contact with people who will suck the faith and positivity out of us. That mindset should not be entertained. Our friends need to speak life or get stepping!

Intercessory Prayers

A number of people in my life stood in the gap for me as I waited on the Lord for my husband, and it was such a comfort. Some of my mentors, girlfriends, and "aunty friends" would call me and just speak God's word over me in a way that never made me feel pressured to marry, but left me encouraged and full of faith.

In July of 2017, my dear friend Tosin—who was already married, by God's grace, and had two beautiful daughters—sent me a message that brought me to tears.

Our pastor, Pastor Sola Olowokere, had held a service titled Miracle Hour for the Unmarried. I couldn't attend because I was out of town for work. Despite being married, Tosin had attended this program for single people, to stand in the gap for me! She shared this message:

Every man is a product of what they think of themselves. Don't see yourself as less than who God has made you. You are a child of God, the apple of His eye. It is a vital position if you want to get anything from God.

You must be in line of location of your destiny.

You won't lose your position or location, in the name of Jesus.

Confess Isaiah 34:15-17. If God ensured that animals had a mate and a family—you are much greater than those animals.

Read 3 John 2 and Genesis 1:26-28. Before Eve existed, she was inside of Adam. Before you were born, you were attached to someone.

Wherever your mate is, they must locate you, because none shall want her mate, according to the scriptures.

Never see yourself not having a chance. (Psalm 34:10)

She also shared these Prayer Points:

1. Father, I thank you for the special plan you have for me and my marital life. I give you all the glory.
2. Father, I know what the book says now, and the book cannot fail, therefore I shall not want my mate.
3. Father, in your mercy, whatever way that I missed my mate, restore me, in the name of Jesus.

I meditated on this message and decreed, day in and day out, that I would not lack my mate. I took those prayer points very seriously and personally.

Tosin's action touched the core of my soul, and I can't put into words how wonderful it felt to know someone was praying and standing in the gap for me, even when I did not know it.

Independent Prayers

In addition to the numerous things I committed to God daily —my health, peace, career, purpose, financial independence and stability, as well as the unending list of family members and friends for whom I interceded—I prayed fervently for my future husband.

Yes, for the husband I did not know, the one I had never seen...yet. The one I called Iremide, "my goodness has come." Boy, I prayed for that man! It was extremely weird, and I even felt odd sharing this with people, because I prayed for him as if he had already come into my life. I was quite detailed and particular with my prayers. I did this because I was certain there was nothing God couldn't do. No matter how big or small my requests were, if it was important to me, then it was important to God. That's how sure I was of God's love for me.

I prayed for his family.

It was very important to me that I married into a Christian family, and one that was close-knit. Every morning as I thanked God for my husband, I would thank him for this man's family. I praised God in advance for depositing a deep and sincere love for me in the heart of each and every one of my in-laws.

I prayed that my husband would have many siblings, because I wanted my children to have many cousins. (Don't ask me why. Lol.) Actually, I know why. I only have one brother, and we are about seven years apart, so we didn't quite grow up together as kids. Though we developed a close relationship in adulthood, I felt like an only child while growing up and became very dependent on friends. As an adult, I was learning how to wisely select friends, that I only needed a few *true* friends, and how to recognize the importance of family. For this reason, I prayed that my husband would have many siblings and a close relationship with them. I also prayed that my kids would have a strong friendship unit within their family and a few good friends.

I prayed that my parents-in-law would view and love me as their child, and I asked for the grace and ability to love them as my parents. I prayed that they would be healthy and be model grandparents to my kids.

I also prayed that my future husband would love his family and mine equally, because I believed that a man who could love both sides of our extended family would be more likely to love his nuclear family.

I prayed about his career.

As I approached a comfortable point in my career, I also prayed about the career of my future husband. I wanted my husband to have, or at least pursue, a professional career. I prayed that he would have steady employment and climb up his professional ladder. Yet, I also prayed he'd have an entrepreneurial mind, so he would not only be great at what he did for the organization he served, but also have the ability to build his own empire.

As funny as it may sound, I prayed that my future husband would be very proficient in the use of Microsoft Office tools, simply because I sometimes struggled with those applications. I would bring home some of my work and try to navigate the intricacies of these tools or struggle with Excel macros and formulas for my budget—thank God for YouTube—so I thought it would be nice if my husband could help me with this.

I prayed about his personality.

I can sometimes be a bit *extra*. I have a lot of energy and can be dramatic. Guys, I can be a whole mood! One fruit of the spirit that I knew I could use more of was patience. I was not in denial of my flaws or the areas in which I needed to improve. I knew I needed a man who would complement me. After all, someone with the same personality might just be a bit too much to handle. So, I prayed that my future husband would be calm and have a warm, soft, and gentle personality—and that he was very patient and tolerant. Gosh, I prayed he would have a double dose of patience!

I prayed that he would be an intelligent person, full of wisdom but also teachable. I prayed for a man who read often, acquired knowledge, and could stimulate my intellect.

At some point, I was into Nollywood. I felt this was a good way for me to pass time, but I didn't want my future home to be a Nollywood center. So, I actually prayed that my future husband wouldn't be as into Nollywood movies as I was, but that he would be diverse in the films he viewed and steer me into consuming more valuable content.

I prayed that my future husband would be neat and clean and have good hygiene, in keeping with the popular phrase, "Cleanliness is next to Godliness."

I prayed he would be a helper, love to cook, have a great sense of humor...and the list went on. Every single detail of my desires, I made known to the manufacturer of this future husband of mine. I withheld nothing, not even the juicy lips and clean nails I wanted him to have!

I prayed about our sex life.

I decided at a very young age that I would have no sex before marriage, but my wait had to be worth it. I won't deny that I am a sexual being, and I desired and was very curious about sex, but not curious enough to break my rule. Since my teenage years, I had felt that if I had sex before marriage, I would get pregnant and obstruct God's plan and purpose for my life.

Though I wouldn't say I encourage this for others, I wanted my future husband to have prior sexual experience. Friends, I prayed about it! (Covers face.) I believed that this would make sex a little less awkward—for me, especially. Although I asked for this, I also prayed passionately that all soul ties from my husband's sexual experiences be broken before he found me—and that *my* breasts and body alone would satisfy him for the rest of our lives. I took this prayer very seriously. I prayed that we would be attracted to each other in every way—physical, sexual, and emotional.

I prayed that sex would be very pleasurable for us, as God intended it to be, and that we would be fruitful, multiply, and replenish the earth.

I prayed about his spirituality.

Above all, I prayed that my future husband would have a burning passion for God through Christ, and that we'd be spiritually yoked and aligned. I prayed that he would have a deep, personal relationship with God and, more importantly, fear God. I believed that having a close relationship with God would help him love me as Christ loves the church, and that this would give him the ability to lead our family according to God's direction. I asked God for a man who would pray for me and with me, so we would have what it takes spiritually to work together to fulfil God's purpose for our lives, marriage, and ministry.

I considered prayers an investment I had to make for my future husband, and I invested all that I could. I took all the risks in this investment, basically praying about anything and everything I could think of. I had read the book *31 Days of Prayer for Your Future Husband: Becoming a Wife Before the Wedding Day,* by Tiffany Machelle Langford. I loved this little book because it covered all the areas of my future husband's life. In it, I could also journal and write blessings over him, trusting God that all those prayers would be answered.

Reflection and Prayer

Today, take some time to go through your prayer lists, no matter how far back you've written. Check off and thank God for the prayers that have been answered. Also update your list and make your new requests known to God with thanks.

CHAPTER 5

PREPARING MYSELF TO BE A GOOD WIFE

Just thinking through the previous chapter made me somewhat dizzy. You may wonder whether all the trouble, prayer, and fasting was even worth it, just because I wanted to get married. A valid question. After all, compared with some of the things people wait on God for—like healing, for instance—this may not seem that serious. But choosing a marriage partner is one of the most important decisions of our lives.

For some people, finding a spouse came super easy, as if they had a flock of husband prospects and just needed to play "Eeny Meeny, Miny, Moe" or flip a coin to pick the best choice. But not everyone has it that easy, so being in tune with the Holy Spirit is crucial, as he will direct each person in the path they should follow.

> *Trust in the Lord with all your heart and lean not on your own understanding; in all your ways submit to him, and he will make your paths straight.*
>
> — PROVERBS 3:5-6 (NIV)

It is important to note, however, that things don't end with praying for and about our future partner—or whatever we are seeking from God. We need to work on ourselves as well, ensuring that we are well equipped to handle whatever it is we are trusting God for. If we are believing for a partner, we also need to make sure our walk with God, character, career, finances, state of well-being, and relationships with others are in check.

The same goes for a person waiting on God for children, jobs, business opportunities, healing, or even clarity of purpose. My wait, of course, was for my husband, so I will share some areas of my life I needed to sort out while I waited. Since I continue to emphasize prayer as an essential ingredient in the process, I'll start with that.

I Prayed for Myself

First, I prayed for the grace and strength to wait well, for the wisdom and clarity of mind to not wallow in sorrow and self-pity. Truthfully, sometimes the wait was painful. Sometimes, I grew lonely, but I knew I needed God's strength to pick myself up when I felt down. I had faith and knew God's word and that he had good plans for me, but sometimes my faith wavered. As a human and emotional being, I accepted the fact that I might feel down, cry, and express how I really felt, but I believed I must not stay sad or spiral into complaining or even depression. I refused to be defeated, but because that is easier said than done, I relied on the grace and strength of God. That is necessary, so we don't remain in sorrow like one who has no hope. We have hope, and our hope is—and always should be—in Christ.

Marriage consists of two imperfect individuals who may come from different backgrounds or be raised in different settings and with different worldviews. The mere nature of being male and female gives each a different perspective. For that reason, it was very important that I was not oblivious to my flaws and imperfections, so I prayed about them. At different points in my life—mid-year, birthdays, the beginning of a new year, or at the time of any remarkable occurrence in my life—I made it a point of duty to do a self-assessment.

I am the first to admit that I'm not perfect at all. I have always been aware that I needed to do better in being patient and soft-spoken. I have a strong personality and am very direct, which is sometimes not well-received, so I knew I needed to do better at being calm and diplomatic in my speech. In certain areas, I tend to be very particular. I had a specific way of doing certain things and always wanted it that way. Also, perhaps because I was from a broken home, I was extremely cautious with guys—a little too snappy and dismissive. I was determined to get it right in the area of marriage at all costs, so I quickly weeded guys out the second I sensed anything contrary to what I wanted.

I consider myself a private person, and I like my personal space to be kept personal...so personal that I did not like anyone lying in my bed. Of course, sometimes I had to share when I had friends come around, and many times I've given up my bed for a guest and slept elsewhere. This is one of the reasons I try not to spend the night outside my home. I always would rather sleep in my own bed, preferably by myself. In fact, that was one fear I had when I thought about being married.

While chatting with my mom one day, I asked if I was weird for not liking to share my bed. She laughed and told me I wouldn't have a choice once I got married.

"You mean, I'll have to share my bed with someone else every single day?" I cringed. "Share my bathroom, kitchen, and closet space, too? The whole entire personal space?"

Guys, I had to take that to the Lord in prayer!

Quite early, as I reflected on my desire to be happily married, I knew that there would be no *me* or *mine* in marriage. I had to pray for the grace to do away with any *me* mentality and shift to a *we* mindset. I prayed for an open and accepting mind, and I really did see God work on me and change me for the better.

The last but biggest of my weaknesses involved the area of

trust. In a number of instances, people who were supposedly very close to me had broken my trust. Though some of their actions did not affect me directly, they caused me to second-guess almost everything, and I struggled with trusting people, especially those closest to me.

After reading all this, you may be thinking, "Whoa, this girl has a lot of issues." You'd be right. In my times of self-reflection, I am still able to admit the areas of my personality that need improvement. This, I believe, is an area in which a lot of people get stuck. Being unable to see your flaws and admit areas where you don't do so well completely cripples any possibility of becoming the best version of yourself. It is in admitting a problem that we can find a solution.

I understand that acceptance can be very difficult, and I always advise the following: When more than one person points out something either positive or negative about you, take some time to evaluate yourself and be truly honest. I am not, by any means, advocating that you let just anyone and everyone label you or judge your character. However, I believe it is in reflecting on yourself, your patterns, and the feedback you receive that you can reach a point of true self-awareness. Then, you can begin to develop improvement plans for the not-so-great areas and maintain or further develop the positives.

With all that in mind, I was very aware of the areas of my personality that needed work, and I prayed seriously about them. With my long list of what I wanted in a husband, I tried to ensure that I was worthy of a man as close to perfect as I desired. In addition to being a helpmate for my husband and being his Proverbs 31 woman, I wanted my personality and countenance to be pleasing to him and everyone around me. I wanted to have a home where peace and love dwelt, a haven for my husband, so I prayed for the fruits of the spirit:

But the fruit of the Spirit is love, joy, peace, forbearance, kindness, goodness, faithfulness, gentleness and self-control. Against such things there is no law.

— GALATIANS 5:22-23 (NIV)

I daily committed my thoughts, actions, and deeds to God's hands and prayed to reflect him in all my doings. I trusted him to fix me where needed, because I know for a fact that attempting to make a change by my own strength or depending on my own abilities would be an epic failure. On my own, I could do nothing, but with Christ, I can do anything. His word confirms this in Philippians 4:13: "I can do all this through him who gives me strength" (NIV).

I didn't rely only on prayers, but also made a conscious effort to be patient, speak more politely, be open to trusting, react better in situations that could trigger me, and just relate better overall to the people around me. In doing this, I saw the hand of God in my life. I celebrated the growth and improvement in myself and in my relationships. I got positive feedback from others, too. I am not perfect, but a work in progress and still striving to be a better version of myself.

I Prayed about My Wedding Day and My Marriage Futuristically

Friends, I am sorry if I am boring you with all these prayers. Many times, even I felt like God must be having a good laugh over some of my requests. But, hey, that's the kind of relationship I have with him. We can talk about anything.

As I shared in the previous chapter, I have a deep love for weddings, so I paid attention to a lot of wedding details. Even without a boyfriend, let alone a fiancé, I had a very intricate wedding plan. I knew I wanted a big, traditional wedding for the sole purpose of honoring my mom and giving her an opportunity to be celebrated, as she has always celebrated with others. I had the colors of my traditional outfits penned down—the soft and dark blue, with a touch of orange in another outfit. I wanted my clothes to be subtle yet tasteful. I also planned to have an intimate but beautiful church wedding, with mostly family and close friends. I really wanted the number of guests to be small.

At about age twenty-six, I started living alone for the first time. I was in a place of contentment, had a great job, and was living in a place I called my Rehoboth (my open space of clarity and solitude). In this phase of my life, I developed a stronger relationship with God. I didn't have distractions, so I often had dialogues with God because I believed that he was living right there with me and that I would hear his responses.

In one of our conversations, about my future partner and my marriage, he told me to sleep.

I was astonished! "Sleep? What do you mean sleep?"

He responded, saying, "Adam was asleep when I formed Eve out of him. I saw it fit that Adam needed a helpmeet for him. Sleep (basically keep your heart at rest) and let me work it out in my own time." (Refer to Genesis 2:21-22 for the story of Eve's creation.)

After that conversation, I looked through the images I had saved and plans I had drafted through the years, some dating back eight years. It seemed almost impossible that I would fail to get married one day. I planned as though I had a partner and a date picked out. My faith level on the matter of marriage was at its peak.

As often as it crossed my mind, I prayed about my wedding vendors, for connections with a great planner, to be favored by everyone who would be working with me, and that my wedding planning—whenever it did happen—would be an enjoyable process for my future husband and me.

The most ridiculous-seeming of my requests was that I would have the wedding of my dreams and it would be at no cost to me. Yes, y'all, I told God I wanted a free, definitely not low-budget, wedding. I laughed at myself sometimes and would say, "I'll let God figure out how he wants to do that." Despite this, it's kind of funny that I always kept a savings account specifically for my wedding. This account grew and grew, yet there was no wedding. I reached out to my friend Tope to get her advice on whether I should just pay off my car with the "wedding fund," considering that I had no potential husband, let alone a wedding to plan.

Tope said, "Pay off your car, and you can start your wedding fund over."

I did just that. When I went to withdraw the cash at the bank, the teller congratulated me and asked when the wedding was. I told her I'd only saved the money by faith but it was coming in handy, now, to pay off my car.

She was so stunned and said, "Not to worry. We can keep your wedding account open, and you can start your savings over. You will eventually have a wedding."

I said *amen* and left the bank. As advised, I started my wedding fund again, but I also made it a serious prayer point that, whatever the case, my wedding would be fully paid for.

I prayed that my wedding would be beautiful, but that my marriage would be even more so. I prayed for our children, our shared purpose, everything that had to do with our future.

I believe in calling things which are not as though they are. For this reason, on many occasions, I would walk down the aisle at my church and envision myself as a bride. My friend and work colleague Priyanka and I would sometimes go pray in the chapel at our place of work. I would have Priyanka play some songs that I had picked out, and I'd walk down the chapel's aisle like a bride. My wedding march song changed often, but on one occasion, it was "This God is too good" by Nathaniel Bassey. The first few lines read:

> I know a God who's merciful and kind
> Faithful and gracious

I'm the apple of his eyes
The thought that fills his heart every morning,
noon, and night.

Every word in that song speaks to my heart, and at this time, it was at the top on my list of the songs I might use when walking down the aisle once my charming prince came along.

Priyanka was always ready to play my track as I walked down the aisle, smiling and waving my hands at my imaginary friends and family. I would finish with a thanksgiving dance in that chapel, just as I hoped I would do on my actual wedding day. It sounds crazy and absurd, I'm sure, but it always felt so real to me.

I thank God for a friend like Priyanka, who never mocked me or considered my actions silly, even though she wasn't raised as a Christian. In fact, she would correct my moves and have me go back to the beginning of the aisle and walk down again. She always expressed admiration for my faith, and we began to pray about things together, as we still do to this day. While I trusted God for a spouse, she was trusting God for children, and every time we went to the chapel, she would ask me to pray with her. This "silly" act of mine began to boost Priyanka's faith and trust in Jesus, and I continue to trust God for her total conversion to Christ and for her miracle children.

Prayer, Prayer, Prayer! It cannot be overemphasized. Prayer works, guys. God listens. We can talk to him about anything, no matter how mundane or ridiculous it may seem. We just have to do our part by trusting God and committing our desires into his hands, having faith that it is done.

It Doesn't End with Prayer, so What's Next?

Do you remember the story of Hannah, the woman at Shiloh? She was childless for many years, and her rival wife taunted her cruelly, rubbing it in and never letting her forget that God had not given her children. This story is elaborated in 1 Samuel 1. I make reference to the story of Hannah because her greatest desire was delayed, she was tortured, and she was not exempt from the background noise. However, at what we might call a conference, a convention, or an annual program, she prayed to God. 1 Samuel calls the event she attended the "annual worship and sacrifice to God-of-the-Angel-Armies." Hannah cried in the sanctuary and lifted her voice to God. 1 Samuel 1:20 tells us that "before the year was out, Hannah had conceived and given birth to a son. She named him Samuel, explaining, 'I asked God for him'" (MSG).

I always found the story of Hannah rather interesting because, considering everything she went through with her rival wife, she must have been mocked by family and friends. She had many reasons to avoid attending the conference that year. She could have easily chosen not to go worship and make sacrifices to God who had not given her a child. She probably would have preferred to avoid any disgrace or insults from other attendees, but she didn't do that. She went to this program and, with a heavy heart, had some one-on-one time with God. The best part for me is that, in that year, God came through for Hannah. Isn't he an amazing God? Indeed, a God of awesome wonders.

Date Nights with God (Conferences, Conventions, Etc.)

While I waited and trusted God for my husband, I didn't just pray. I believe that "[...] faith without works is dead" (James 2:20 NKJV). I opted to not just meet or commune with God in my personal space or at random times as my spirit felt the need, but I met with him at several annual church programs. My home church—RCCG, Strong Tower parish, now known as Christ Family Kingdom Center—held some major conferences. We have the Solution Conference around March, Impact Convention sometime in October, and twelve days of prayer and fasting in December. But my favorite of them all was the Praise

Festival in November. The Redeemed Christian Church of God, North America also held the annual Festival of Life convention in July and, I believe, a convention for the unmarried sometime in June. I must say, we had lots of opportunities throughout the year to have some fine dining on spiritual food with God.

Just as Hannah and her family in 1 Samuel attended the annual worship service in Shiloh, I tried to attend some of the annual programs listed above, but not for the sole purpose of looking for a spouse. To me, they served as an opportunity to meet and fellowship with God in an unusual way and in a different space. At most of these programs, we had guest ministers—great men and women of God from other churches or Christian organizations—so it was an opportunity to hear God's word through other prophets and from different perspectives.

Hallelujah Challenge: Olowogbogboro

In June of 2017, there was a trend on Instagram (a social networking service) called the Hallelujah Challenge. I came across it a number of times, saw the posts and hashtags, but didn't quite follow. One day, just out of curiosity, I decided to see what this challenge was all about. Hosted by Nigerian gospel artist Nathaniel Bassey, it was basically an hour-long midnight virtual praise challenge, and it was supposed to go on for thirty days. Since the challenge was based in Nigeria, it would begin at 6:00 pm for me in America.

I was a few days late to the game, but boy, oh boy, I was hooked from the first day I tuned in. It was an unexplainable experience. All we did was sing and praise for an hour, but somehow, I ended up on the floor of my living room, worshiping and crying profusely. It felt like heaven on Earth, and I heard God tell me he needed that hour with me for the remainder of the challenge.

I have always cultivated an atmosphere of praise and

worship. That is the ministry God called me to serve in from a young age, but this went deeper. I truly felt God's presence joining the Hallelujah Challenge daily. The atmosphere was always charged.

We proclaimed "Just Like That" miracles, declaring that the things we had been looking to God for would happen "just like that." It became a mantra, a hashtag, a declaration, and people began to share testimonies of things turning around "just like that," miracles happening "just like that," and healings happening "just like that." Through the remaining days of the challenge, I praised God with everything in me, I danced like David danced, I sang till I almost lost my voice sometimes, and every day, I wrote down one thing I was trusting God for. Of course, my husband was front row on that list, and I believed it would happen "just like that."

The challenge ended for me on a very high note. I was filled and satisfied with the Holy Spirit, full of faith, and more confident than ever that "Olowogbogboro"—God, whose mighty hand can reach any length, had turned things around for my good.

Praise Festival

I am a praise fanatic. Praise is one of the things I love to do the most, and I don't get tired of doing it. I can praise even when I cannot pray. It is what God requires from us. We were created for this one purpose, to praise him, and that is why this annual praise festival remains my favorite meet-up spot with God.

In addition to my love for praise, I continue to look forward to this program because God has, time and time again, answered every request that I have tendered to him. I have tears in my eyes just reflecting on the many testimonies that have come out of this annual program. At a particular praise festival, my ultimate request was granted, but we will discuss that in more detail later.

I attended various conferences to ensure that I was feeding my mind with God's word, working on myself, and waiting on the manifestation of my miracles according to God's standard and not the world's. It was very important to me that my husband found me in God's way, at God's time, and in his will. It was very rare that you would find me in a club or other spots with the sole purpose of meeting a man. I didn't want to ever take credit or give credit to any individual, website, or social gathering for my miracle and testimony of marriage. All the credit, all of the glory, had to go to God. No one was to share in it.

So, in addition to praying and having faith, I continued to seek God's presence, meeting with him at different events and, with a heart full of praise and thanks, making my requests known to him.

I Read and Consumed Content on Marriage

It is extremely important to learn and get well-educated on anything you are aspiring to become. For example, if you want to start a business, you don't wake up and just dive into it. You do extensive research, ask questions, shadow people already in the business, acquire knowledge, read books, and do whatever it takes to be well prepared and equipped before getting into it. The same applies in preparing for marriage. It is important to be educated about the institution of marriage and understand what it takes to be happy and successful in a marriage. It is also important to understand how to truly be ready and properly positioned to find your partner or be found.

As I dove into the subject, I noticed some common key factors in all the books I read and from the speakers I listened to on various platforms. It was almost like everyone was saying the same thing but in different ways. I learned that, in order to be successful as a wife, I had to be prayerful, master putting God first in all I do, and let God be the sole director of my life.

I learned that I needed to have my own resources and money, as well as to be accomplished, well-rounded, and successful independently. A woman was made to be a helpmate for a man, not a liability to him.

I discovered the importance of abstinence from sex. I learned that sex is a powerful, unexplainable, spiritual connection between a man and woman within the confines of marriage. Being sexual outside of marriage not only displeases God, but it results in forming a spiritual bond or soul tie with a person in a relationship outside of God's will. This tie could linger into marriage. Unplanned pregnancies, sexually transmitted diseases, increased promiscuity, abortion, and even a sense of loneliness or emptiness can result from having sex before marriage.

> *Flee from sexual immorality. All other sins a person commits are outside the body, but whoever sins sexually, sins against their own body. Do you not know that your bodies are temples of the Holy Spirit, who is in you, whom you have received from God? You are not your own; you were bought at a price. Therefore honor God with your bodies.*
>
> — 1 CORINTHIANS 6:18-20 (NIV)

> *Now for the matters you wrote about: "It is good for a man not to have sexual relations with a woman." But since sexual immorality is occurring, each man should have sexual relations with his own wife, and each woman with her own husband.*
>
> — (1 CORINTHIANS 7:1-2 NIV)

I read a book on love languages for singles, which I found extremely beneficial because I never knew that each person had a peculiar way in which they want to be loved. Without that understanding, what we project to others in order to demonstrate our love may not be perceived as a show of love.

The biggest revelation I got in preparing for marriage related to the topic of submission and the concepts of love and respect. Just like most unmarried people, I had it all wrong. There is a preconceived notion that women literally must bow to their husbands, have no say in the marriage, and are pretty much enslaved, for lack of a better word. All lies! In reading and learning, I grew to understand the true meaning of submission, which really involves deferring to the decision of the husband in a situation where the husband and wife are unable to agree. The woman submits to her husband's authority or decision, but it does not end there. She is expected to pray to God that whatever decision the husband has made will be directed by the Holy Spirit and be in accordance with God's will.

A Godly woman will not struggle much in advising and helping her husband in decision-making, since he will trust her judgment. In a case where opinions absolutely differ and a compromise cannot be reached, a Godly man will always seek to be led by God to do whatever is best for the family and is pleasing in God's sight.

For this reason, I considered it extremely crucial that I marry a man who honored and feared the Lord. Feeding on God's word and ideas for marriage was a great preparation technique.

I only read books that were Christian-based, because I was trying to prepare myself for a Christian marriage. I also enjoyed YouTube vlogs. Some of my favorites were Ayo and Ope Davies, Heather and Cornelius Lindsey, and Tolulope Solutions. I listened to several messages by T. D. Jakes, Funke Adejumo, Myles Munroe, Joyce Myers, Joel Osteen, Mike and Natalie Todd, and my home pastor, Sola Olowokere.

You can find a wealth of information and content out there that would really help in preparing for the lifelong institution of marriage. It is best to learn and prepare during the waiting period, have an idea of what to expect, and learn of some ways to handle the ups and downs. Please note that reading and learning will not necessarily make you perfect for marriage or automatically make your future marriage problem-proof. That's not the idea or promise at all. Feeding your mind with the right information and ideas on how to prepare for marriage can *help* you become an ideal candidate for matrimony. It can also help you enter your future marriage with better understanding of your spouse and of God's ways. Preparing ahead will foster a healthy love and lasting marriage and make matters much easier than if you try to learn and figure out the institution while already in it.

Reflection and Prayer

Think of simple measures you have taken that have resulted in testimonies. Thank God for the wisdom to make those little moves.

CHAPTER 6

INVESTING IN MYSELF

Our spiritual state is only the first step in positioning ourselves for the miracle we are waiting for. We also need to make investments in our "natural" condition.

I Invested in My Education and Career

My family background, to a large extent, shaped my thoughts and views on education and its importance. When I was growing up, my grandma often said that all her children and grandchildren must be educated. Since she had ended her education at the primary level, it was paramount to her that the next generation would do better in that regard and possibly attain the highest level of education. We heard this so many times, it became a blueprint for our futures. Above all, I knew I had to go to school and strive for success.

My mom was also an extreme influence on this aspect of my life. She was very career-driven and professional. I watched her work tirelessly while we were growing up, just so my brother and I could have the best education. We attended excellent schools, and Mom invested in additional tutorials for us. Honestly, at the time, I thought she was just plain mean, because we had to go for group tutoring after school. By the time we came home from our lessons, a home tutor would be waiting for us, and when Mom returned from work, she would start *her* round of tutoring. Education was no joke, I tell you.

When I was sixteen, I moved back to the US and lived with my uncle and aunt in Minnesota while I attended a community college for two years. After that, I was off to a university that was far from their home. Although I was away from adult influence, renting an apartment with a college mate, I saw value in how I was brought up. However, this lack of guidance and supervision made career decisions a little difficult.

During my time at the community college, I worked on campus as a student ambassador and as a mentor with Upward Bound, which was a mentorship program for high school students. I also worked as a pharmacy technician at Walgreens Pharmacy because I wanted to be a pharmacist.

That career goal was another area of my life in which I experienced delay, but this one led to disappointment, time and time again. I needed to pass Organic Chemistry I and II in order to complete my undergraduate degree. I also needed to have a passing score in these courses to be considered for any pharmacy school, but I continued to fail them. I did everything I could—worked with tutors after school, locked myself in the room to study for tests, and joined study groups with classmates. I would feel hopeful and confident when it was time for the exam, but every time I got my results, I received a failing grade.

After about two years at the community college, I transferred to St Cloud State University to complete my undergraduate degree. I attempted the organic chemistry courses again and still failed. Despite the extreme frustration this caused, I couldn't imagine letting go of my desire to be a pharmacist.

While in school, I volunteered at St Cloud Hospital and was miraculously offered a job as an admitting clerk at the hospital's Emergency and Trauma Center. I say *miraculously* because I honestly do not remember applying or interviewing for the job. I just remember getting a call with the offer, and poof! There I was, in my scrubs, admitting patients into the ER. I worked there till I graduated from the university and for a few months afterward.

As graduation neared, my university advisor counselled me to consider changing my major. Though I had all the other courses necessary to graduate, I couldn't do so without passing Organic Chemistry. Eventually, I was allowed to walk in the graduation ceremony, but was told I wouldn't get my diploma until I had passed those two courses.

I cried profusely on my graduation day, because I still had those courses hanging over me, which meant I really hadn't graduated. My mom flew in from Nigeria to attend my graduation, and the family threw me a graduation party, which I greatly appreciated, but it made me feel worse. I wasn't sure what direction my life would take after this day. I called Mimi that night and just cried.

While working at the hospital, I had met many healthcare professionals who were not doctors, nurses, or pharmacists. There were hospital managers, project managers, healthcare administrators, operations managers, etc. Although I hadn't quite given up on pharmacy, I began to have hope that there were other careers I could pursue and be successful at.

Segi, a friend from church who was like a big sister, referred me for a job with Minnesota Oncology as a medical records specialist. I applied and, when I eventually was offered the job, I relocated to the twin cities. That was when I felt I had officially adopted a career path in healthcare. While working, I decided to try Organic Chemistry for the last time at Metropolitan Community and Technical College. I made up my mind that if I didn't pass this time, then it was not God's will for my life. Let's just say, my desire to be a pharmacist didn't align with God's career path for me.

I had plans to further my education beyond my

undergraduate degree, but that was not pressing since I was still getting established in corporate America. I worked with Minnesota Oncology for almost two years, until I got laid off. I felt like my whole life was crashing before my eyes. I was helpless and didn't know what to do. For weeks, I would still get ready in the morning, as though I was going to work, and drive to my friend Mimi's Jewelry store. I started filling a vending machine in her store with pop and water, and that was the source of my weekly paycheck for a while—until the Holy Spirit gave me a nudge.

As days and weeks went by, God continued to remind me that I had plans to get my master's degree. This was the perfect opportunity, since I wasn't working. Every step of the way, God directed me. His voice was loud and clear. A thought that had never crossed my mind dropped in my heart, to explore universities in London. I found myself researching universities in London that offered a master's program in healthcare management. I applied to three schools and, after I got rejected by the second, I asked God if I'd misheard him. I was beginning to get discouraged and started losing hope.

I switched gears and looked into schools in Minnesota. Then, to my greatest surprise, I got an email with an acceptance offer from the University of Surrey, UK. I cried, ecstatic and full of gratitude to God. He'd ordered my steps through the entire process.

With renewed confidence, I called St. Cloud State University and told them I'd accept a diploma in Biology, even though I had all the courses for Biomedical Sciences except for Organic Chemistry. I was ready to follow God's direction, accept his will for my life, and move forward. With all the joy and peace in my heart, I finally received my undergraduate degree, had gained some work experience, and was now heading for my master's program. Without discussing it with anyone but God, I applied for a student visa, applied for financial aid, and secured student housing. When I broke the news of my departure to friends and family, it was well received. For me, that was the final indication that God was totally involved.

By God's grace, all my courses went well. I didn't fail any class, and soon enough, I was back in Minnesota, wrapping up my dissertation and getting ready for graduation. One of the most remarkable moments in my life was the day I handed in my final dissertation. I cried happy tears of relief and accomplishment. I could hardly believe that just in the next few months after submitting my dissertation, I would officially be a master's degree holder. To this day, that remains one of my biggest accomplishments, mainly because I can only ascribe the glory to God. All my help, guidance, and direction came solely from him. While I wrote my dissertation, I worked with my uncle and aunt who run a home healthcare agency.

I eventually furthered my career at Unitedhealth Group, continuing to learn, leveraging my previous experiences, and trying not to get too comfortable. I pushed for growth in my career, delved into business analysis in the healthcare domain, and got a job at one of America's best healthcare institutions, Mayo Clinic. My job at Mayo Clinic required me to move to Rochester, Minnesota. In addition to the magnificent career growth and advancement, this move was the beginning of my breakthrough in all areas of my life.

How did I find myself at Mayo Clinic? It's an interesting story. Femi, who I talked about in Chapter 3, had told me he got a job there and would be moving to Minnesota. Since I was also job-searching at that time, I decided to try applying there. That was the best career move I've made to this day. I guess remaining friends with Femi wasn't all bad.

As I'm writing this, I've worked at Mayo Clinic for over five years and, to Gods glory, am thriving in my career—not as a pharmacist, but walking the path that God knew was best. I have been intentional about growth and advancement, though gradually, ensuring that I do not become stagnant.

While I worked as a business analyst, I enrolled in a prep

course at Rochester Community College to become a project management professional. What an overwhelming time! I attended class at night, worked on assignments, stayed caught up on voluminous reading, and still had to be functional at work. It was no joke.

After long nights of class, studying, taking practice tests, and what have you, I failed the Project Management Professional (PMP) exam. I called my mom, crying because I couldn't deal with the thought of having to study for the exam all over again. Before I took the exam—not knowing I would fail, of course—I had planned a small birthday lunch for my friend Sayo. I was ready to call the few invited guests and tell them the lunch was canceled, because I was too sad to socialize. But the more I beat myself up over the failure, the more God comforted me, and I started to look at the lunch in a positive light. It would help me get my mind off my temporary failure.

When the weekend came, I braced myself, met up with friends, and shook it off. I took a two-month break from studying and anything related to PMP. I went about my life and, after my break, dusted my books off and began studying again. I gave it my absolute best and committed my efforts to God's hands, reminding him that I was doing this because I wanted growth in my career. God honored my request. When I took the exam again, I aced it!

A few months later, I interviewed for my same Senior Business Analyst role at Mayo but also explored a different department. Instead of being offered the position I applied for, I was offered the Project Manager position that had opened up in the department.

You may wonder how all these stories apply to having faith and waiting on God. I strongly believe it is essential that, while waiting for a spouse or whatever your "wait case" is, you do not become idle or complacent. Develop yourself in whatever capacity you can, whether in your education, business, talent, career, etc. Often, marriage can delay or hinder some of a person's goals and achievements because, when you cleave to your partner, it is no longer about you alone.

Even when you fail, even when you get rejected, even when it seems like everything keeps crumbling, don't quit. Sulk if you need to, but don't dwell in that space. Dust yourself off and try again. No matter the situation, hold onto God's word that you can do all things

I Invested in My Finances

I am very big on savings. No matter how much or little I earn, I must give, and I must save. Many times, others have thought I was being cheap or frugal, but that never really mattered to me. I try to stick to a budget and live within my means. Years ago, I made it a point in life to ensure that I was financially secure and independent. I never wanted to be a liability to any man, or anyone else. Instead, I've always aspired to be a blessing and a "lender to nations," as the Bible says in Deuteronomy 15:16 (NLT), so I was very intentional with my finances. By God's grace, I didn't—and still don't—have any credit card debts. Don't get me wrong, I have credit cards but spend only what I am able to immediately pay off. Life is already crazy enough, and I didn't want to further complicate things by carrying a burden of debt.

To be honest, I like the finer things in life. I admire them and people who can afford nice things. Living in a country like America, where every retail store is practically waving a credit card in your face, it takes divine intervention to resist temptation. As much as I loved nice things, I was able to turn away from excessive and unnecessary shopping. If I did buy something expensive, I shopped for the best deals on the item and, most importantly, made sure I had the cash at hand. When I traveled, the duty-free option was my best friend. It allowed me to buy some things at a discounted price, but I never bought what I couldn't afford.

When my car became so old its wheels were all but falling off, I longed to buy a Range Rover Sport. I loved the car and felt it would suit me. Two of my uncles drove Range Rovers, and every time I got in one, I would imagine how cute I would look in the Sport model. Guys, when the hour came that I needed to finally buy a new car, and I weighed my bank account against the cost of a Range Rover Sport—the cost of any new car at all, actually—and the number of years it would take me to pay it off, I had to give myself a very good talk. I borrowed myself some brain and made myself rethink my choice of a car. I spent a lot more time thinking about what my basic needs in a car really were. Honestly, even a tricycle would have worked. I didn't need a luxury car and started looking for affordable options.

Like I do about everything that pertains to my life, big or small, I prayed for God's direction on the best choice for me and asked for complete peace over whatever decision I made. I had been sharing my car hunt frustrations with my friend Tope. It really was a struggle, since I know so little about cars. Tope offered to go car window-shopping with me one Saturday morning, and our trip ended with me driving a brand-new Nissan Altima, with payments I could afford. By God's grace, I paid it off in eighteen months. I still consider that one of the best decisions I've made—no hiccups, no issues whatsoever.

My savings came in super handy for this, as I mentioned earlier. Although I was as single as single could be, I'd saved for my wedding. Those funds enabled me to quickly pay off my car. I also saved for a home, had a 401k, and invested in stocks and bonds.

The moral here isn't to avoid buying anything, deny yourself nice things, or not spend at all. Far from it! I've spent and *still* spend a lot of money. When I was single, I bought nice things, gave to others, and indulged here and there, but I tried to ensure that it was within my means. When the right man came along, I didn't want to be a financial burden, but a value add. I was, in essence, practicing how to manage finances for when I'd eventually get married and start a family.

Here are some of the scriptures that influenced my decisions in this area:

- Romans 13:8 (NIV): "Let no debt remain outstanding except the continuing debt to love one another, for whoever loves others has fulfilled the law."
- Proverbs 27:12 (NIV): "The prudent see danger and take refuge, but the simple keep going and pay the penalty."
- Proverbs 21:20 (NIV): "The wise store up choice food and olive oil, but fools gulp theirs down."

I Made a Change in My Health and Lifestyle

For as long as I can remember, I have been on the heavy side. I never really considered myself overly obese, but I was the biggest in my circle of friends, weight-wise. It had been that way since I was in high school, so it was just the norm for me. I ate with no care in the world, always had all my meals for the day and snacks in between. If I missed a meal, I would ensure that I made up for it. On some of my morning drives to work, I would stop at McDonalds to get a large Iced Coffee with twelve creams and twelve sugars. Ridiculous, I know. It didn't stop there. I would top that coffee off with a sausage and egg McGriddle, sometimes two. I lived a very sedentary life. I sat at a desk for long hours at work, and once I got home, I was back in the chair or on my sofa.

At every annual physical appointment, I received a clean bill of health. The doctor would always advise that I work on losing weight, but since everything was fine, I didn't make it a priority. Every now and then, I signed up at the gym and spent some time on the treadmill, but I was never consistent. After a few months, I would get lazy and quit. For many years, this was the pattern, and my weight fluctuated like a yoyo.

While I was studying in London, I was the most active, since I had to do a lot of walking to catch the bus or hop on the train. I also joined a gym and was more motivated to go because a friend would go with me. I cooked healthy meals and was more conscious about my well-being. All this came to a pause once I returned to the US, as I went back to being inconsistent with my diet and exercise.

This went on until the summer of 2018, when Mimi got married and I was her Maid of Honor. My outfits were tailormade and fit me wonderfully. I felt beautiful and was so focused on carrying out my Maid of Honor duties, I had no concerns about my looks...until a few months later, when the wedding pictures and videos came out. I did *not* like the image of myself in those.

How had I let myself get so big? At this time, I weighed about 196 lbs., which was certainly obese and unhealthy. I pondered on it but didn't take any action until September 30th, a night I will never forget. I woke up at midnight and dropped flat on the floor to speak to God about my plans to lose weight and begin living a healthy lifestyle. I told him that my body was his temple and dwelling place and I desired to keep it holy. I admitted that, on my own and by my strength, I couldn't accomplish this goal; but, by his Grace and strength, I most certainly could attain any health goal and surpass it. With my metabolism and the tendency to easily gain weight due to my genetics, what I needed was not a quick fix, a change for looks alone, or a crash diet. I needed a complete, permanent lifestyle change, and I certainly couldn't give that to myself by my own strength.

I committed my plans to God, because he created me and formed every part of me, and it would only be by his grace that I could get where I desired to be. I thanked God and, on October

I, started off greatly cutting down on my carbs, keeping track of everything I ate, and counting my calories. I joined the gym at work and would attend short exercise sessions. I would walk during my breaks and ensure I had a minimum of 10,000 steps daily, which I later increased to 15,000 and to 20,000. From deep within me, I felt brand new. I felt so alive. God had given me control over that part of my life. Slowly, the weight dropped off, and I ended up losing over forty pounds, which was way more than I set out to lose.

People speculated that I was using supplements, was on a keto-diet, and so on. At first, I would explain, because I wanted them to understand that I'd worked so hard to get where I was. God quickly reminded me that it was not my efforts, it was his grace that helped. For that, I could take no credit and owed no one an explanation. I was and still am extremely grateful to God and absolutely in love with my body and lifestyle. Those truths were all that mattered, not the thoughts and opinions of other people.

My joy grew even more full when, during my next physical exam, my doctor expressed how highly impressed she was with my current weight and how healthy I was, in general. This made me happy, because it was a fulfillment of scripture in my life. "Beloved, I wish above all things that thou mayest prosper and be in health, even as thy soul prospereth" (3 John 1:2 KJV).

God gave me the wisdom to take advantage of my time of singleness to adopt a healthy lifestyle that is permanent. I am glad that, for me, it was not about being sexy, slim, vain, appealing to the images that social media approves of, or trying to impress a man. At that time, I was at the peak of singleness, so there was no guy or prospect to impress. It really was for me, my health, and "[...] presenting (my) body as a living sacrifice, holy, pleasing to God—that is (my) true and proper worship" (Romans 12:1 NIV). God also used this change to prepare my body for my future husband, for childbearing, and all that's related.

I Travelled, Learned New Skills, and Had Fun

Since I *knew* I would one day be married, have children, and be responsible for my family, I was certain that there would come a time when it might not be as easy to just stop everything and go on a trip, or spread my wings and fly in other ways. The time for that was during my singleness. As my finances and work schedule permitted, I travelled. This included a number of girl trips, family vacations, road trips, holiday trips, and whatever trip came up.

While studying in London, I went to Paris with my cousin and her friends. Over Christmas, I went with my uncle who lived in London and his family to Tenerife, Spain. After I moved back to the US, the following year, my same family in London invited me for a quick vacation in Malaga. Without thinking twice, I boarded a plane to London to catch up with them and head to Malaga.

I always wanted to go to Dubai, and I started looking into it. I reached out to my friends Jumoke and Dolapo, who were also down for a trip, and off we went. While there, Jumoke and I decided to make a day stop in Turkey.

Later, I came across some great cruise deals to the Bahamas, too great a deal to resist. I sent a message to see how my friend Tosin felt about a trip and, without any hesitation, she sent me her portion of the cruise fare. I asked Mimi as well, and before we knew it, we were having the time of our lives on a cruise ship.

One Thursday night, Mimi called and asked me to drive to Chicago with her, which was about seven hours away, so we could attend a comedy show the next day. I moaned and whined, but after a lot of convincing, I was on board. The next day, we cruised down to Chi-town.

I could go on and on about the various abrupt trips I went on, making wonderful memories and just enjoying life, but I also planned travel in advance. I made it an annual tradition to visit my friend Simi and her family in Canada. Her son's birthday and mine are one day apart, and it was nice to celebrate with them. I also ended up making several other wonderful friends there.

Travel wasn't the only opportunity my singleness afforded me. One of the things I'm most proud of is that, as a fully grown adult, I decided to take up swimming. I didn't like being restricted to chilling by the poolside when on vacation. I also wanted to at least know how to swim before I got married, so I could swim while on my honeymoon. So, I signed up for a swimming class and overcame my fear of being in the water. That made my travels a lot more fun! When I was on holiday from then on, I was *in* the pool swimming. When I go to the beach, I at least try to get a little wet. It may sound really mundane, but learning to swim as an adult remains one of my big achievements.

Since I'm a member of my church choir, I thought it would be nice to develop my musical abilities—not to just work on my vocals, but learn an instrument. After making some inquiries, I found a private piano tutor. I took piano lessons for a few months and learned the basics. I was greatly enjoying it and don't quite remember the cause of my break in transmission, but I kind of let my learning fall through the cracks.

The moral of this part of the story is that the best time to have fun, travel, learn new skills, and do some of the things you love or are scared to do is when you are single. There is just a bit more time, freedom, and flexibility. I had some of the best times of my life, adventures and experiences I wouldn't trade for anything.

I am not in any way implying that marriage or family equate to bondage. It just may not be as easy to do those things afterward, since life will no longer be about *me* anymore but *us*. Others require our consideration when attempting to do these things, then. I was intentional about making the best of my time as a single lady, and it built my anticipation to create even more exciting memories and experiences with my future husband and our children.

The wait time is the perfect opportunity to ensure that you are growing and functioning at your best. The flipside is to let years pass you by, simply because you are waiting for marriage. Instead, focus on achieving your goals and have fun. This is the time when you get to be selfish, for lack of a better word, making the best of your life and setting yourself up for a great future.

Reflection and Prayer

Make a list of personal goals you would like to achieve. Break them down into different areas of life: career, health, spiritual, etc. Give yourself a realistic timeframe to achieve these goals and, with the list in your hand, surrender all your plans to God. Ask him for guidance, direction, and everything you need to accomplish each goal.

CHAPTER 7

JUST WHEN I WASN'T LOOKING

Thanksgiving will always be my favorite holiday, and I will tell you why. You might want to get a refill on your tea, soda, or water; top up your popcorn; sit back; and relax. It's story time, y'all!

So, it was a regular day at work, and my friend Tosin texted, asking what plans I had for Thanksgiving, which was right around the corner. I told her I had nothing major planned, other than the family tradition of gathering at my oldest uncle's house.

She replied, "I was thinking we should have a small dinner on Friday. I just feel God has been the realest this year! Mimi got married, Ify (another friend) got married, you got a promotion, amongst other things."

Mind you, Tosin and her family had just moved into their new home, so I was ready to get this party started! Tosin was assigned to finding us a restaurant, I would create an invite, and we would get a few of our friends together. We called it *Friendsgiving.*

During the week leading up to our Friendsgiving dinner, we had just wrapped up thirty-six solid hours of praise at the annual praise festival I mentioned in Chapter 6, and I was looking forward to some good rest over the Thanksgiving break. Like me, most of my friends had multiple dinners to hop through on Thursday, Thanksgiving Day. I had a birthday party to attend over the weekend, as well. This made me have second thoughts about holding the Friendsgiving dinner on Friday, as it was beginning to feel like we had a whole lot going on. I asked Tosin what she thought about us canceling dinner, but her answer was a big fat, "No!" So, I braced myself and began to look forward to an eventful Thanksgiving celebration.

Friendsgiving

On Thanksgiving, I drove down from Rochester to the Twin Cities, had an amazing time with family and friends, and ate— but not too much. After all was done, I passed the night at my brother's apartment.

The next day, I didn't have much planned other than to rest in, go for a walk in the mall, and get ready for our Friendsgiving dinner at six that evening. I was lounging on my airbed when my brother told me something had gone wrong with the apartment building's furnace, and the hot water wasn't running. It was extremely cold outside, so the water running in was icy. We managed to brush our teeth and hoped that the issue would be resolved by evening.

I devised a backup plan. If the water wasn't fixed, I would pack a bag with all I needed for dinner and, after my walk at the mall, head over to Mimi's apartment to shower and get ready, since she lived just a few minutes from the mall. It wasn't unusual for me to spend the night or shower at Mimi's apartment, since I lived so far away. My trips to the Twin Cities usually spanned a weekend, so I stayed with her and, after she got married, with my brother.

While I was walking in the mall, I got a message from Mimi, letting me know her husband, ID, had a friend visiting. The rest of the message read, "The guy is very cute. No wedding ring but doesn't live in Minnesota. I have to hear his accent, though. He may move back to Minnesota once he finishes grad school. He even has a dimple. He is coming to dinner tonight. I invited him."

After a good laugh, a little confusion, and more laughs, I asked if she could take a picture and if English was his downfall. I basically wanted to know if he spoke good English because it's one of the details Mimi pays attention to.

She said she couldn't take a picture because he was observant and would notice. Her response regarding his English was just hilarious. I told her to let me know when he was gone so I could go over and shower. I honestly didn't take the conversation seriously. It just really cracked me up, a much-needed comic relief, and I continued to enjoy my walk.

After a couple hours, I let Mimi know I was heading over to shower. She said that her husband's friend was still around, but time was running out. As one of the hosts of the dinner, I couldn't be late. That was all I could think about. Mimi left the apartment door open for me, and I went right into my self-appointed room to get organized. I heard voices in the living room, exchanging goodbyes. Finally! ID's friend left. I jumped into the shower, and we got ready for dinner.

I know the story is getting long, but hang in there. It's about to get interesting.

Rendezvous at the Restaurant

As our few guests begin to trickle into the Italian restaurant we'd reserved for dinner, we exchanged pleasantries, took our coats off, and tried to get situated.

Mimi suddenly exclaimed, "ID's friend is here!" She was all jittery as she introduced him to Tosin and me.

I said a quick *hello*, but didn't quite catch his name. Getting somewhat irritated at Mimi's overexcitement, I set my things down and headed to use the restroom.

Of course, Mimi followed me to the restroom and asked, "So, what do you think?"

"Mimi," I said, "can you stop and let me pee in peace?" I hoped she'd gotten the message that a hook-up or guy assessment was the least of my priorities that night. To make matters worse, nothing about this guy stood out or caught my attention, so I didn't quite understand Mimi's excitement about him.

Once we all settled down, I started talking with a sweet couple I'd invited, Tobi and his beautiful wife Lara. Tobi was my classmate in high school, and we had recently reconnected at church after so many years. I introduced Tobi and Lara to everyone at the table, then ID's friend introduced himself as "Sun-me."

We all had a good laugh over how he'd pronounced his name, and he clarified that his name was Sanmi, Oluwasanmi in his Yoruba dialect.

We ordered a variety of entrees to share, ate, and chatted the night away. As we wrapped up dinner, Tosin reminded us of the purpose for which we were gathered, which was to express our gratitude to God for all the amazing things he had done for each of us throughout the year.

Fourteen of us had gathered at the dinner table that night, and it was beautiful to hear what each person was thankful for. ID created a burst of emotion when he sang a song of gratitude for his marriage to Mimi that year. Ify and Kenyeh were also thankful for their marriage and a successful wedding. Tope shed tears, in awe of God for how he had helped her and greatly improved her son's speech. Each person had a beautiful testimony to share, but one shook the table, Oluwasanmi's.

I was vaguely paying attention, since he sat farther down the table from me, but I heard him thank God for bringing him close to the completion of his master's program in Boston. He was going to be done in the coming month. He went on to thank God by faith that, in the coming year, he would also have a fiancée and be getting married. As he spoke, he was gesticulating and ended up pointing in my direction.

The whole room went crazy. Everyone started cheering and screaming and clapping. I was beyond embarrassed, flushed, confused, and speechless, all at the same time. Oluwasanmi didn't let the chaos stop him. He was sweating profusely but carried on with his reasons for gratitude.

By the time it was my turn to share what I was thankful for, I was still embarrassed. I shared my gratitude to God for helping me accomplish the career goals I had set that year and for blessing me with a project management position at work. I also thanked God in advance for my husband and future marriage. Since we had celebrated a number of new marriages that year, it was only right that I tapped into the blessing. Everyone cheered, and we moved on.

It was a fantastic, memorable night, and we gathered for pictures. Sanmi came and stood right beside me. While we took pictures with Mimi, ID, and another friend of ID's, I thought, *Now, he has gotten ideas.* As we left, I was very glad we hadn't canceled the dinner. It gave me so much joy to see how happy and thankful everyone was.

Reflection and Prayer

In your current state, think of some things and/or people you are thankful for:

Father I thank you for: _____.

CHAPTER 8

GOOD THING WE HAD
DINNER

You are probably wondering what happened after Friendsgiving dinner. Well, the night ended, but the story did not.

The next evening, which was a Saturday, I went to Mimi's apartment to hang out for a while. ID had just returned from visiting with his boys, and out of nowhere I said jokingly, "Hope you invited my husband to your hangout."

He laughed. "I did, actually, but he was a no-show. I wasn't able to reach him on the phone, either." He paused and looked at me. "I also invited him to church tomorrow."

Not the response I'd expected, considering I asked as a joke. We watched a movie, and I went back to my brother's apartment.

On Sunday, I was walking the hallway at church before service started and ran into ID. As usual, he pulled me to the corner so we could chat. ID and I are such close friends that, as an inside joke, our group calls Mimi his main wife and me the assistant wife. Evidently, the sisterhood Mimi and I share transferred to her husband. But I digress. So, as ID and I chatted, I joked again and asked, "Has my husband come to church?" obviously referring to Sanmi.

"He couldn't attend," ID said. "Didn't have a ride or

something." ID then explained that he and Sanmi were close family friends and, though he spoke highly of Sanmi's family, he hadn't interacted with Sanmi much because he lived in Boston. "I just don't think Sanmi could be your type, based on the guys you've said are attractive in the movies we've watched together."

I couldn't believe my ears and found the comment hilarious, but I understood how ID could have made such an assumption. I did tend to express attraction for the "bad boys," but that was never a determining factor of the type of guy I would actually date. They were too likely to cheat on a girl. I clarified this for ID, and he said he would speak to Sanmi to see where his head was with regards to dating.

I made it very clear to ID that I was not expressing interest in Sanmi, though I was always open to making friends and didn't judge based on just looks. I also let him know I wasn't at all desperate for a relationship, as my focus was now on improving myself. We had an interesting conversation until it was time for service.

After church, I began my ninety-five mile drive home to Rochester. It was nice to get back after a very long and eventful weekend. I put my things away and prepared for the week. After getting settled, I was relaxing on the couch and texting with Mimi about some church activity when my phone rang. Why was ID calling?

"I need to ask you a question urgently," he said. "Sanmi wants to go see you in Rochester tomorrow before he travels back to Boston. Is that okay?"

"Heck no," I said, confused, since there was no backstory. I know I had been joking about this guy, but I certainly wasn't expecting or preparing for a visit. "I will be busy at work tomorrow," I said, "so Sanmi can't come."

ID asked if it was at least okay for him to give Sanmi my number.

I said, "Give it to him if you think it's a good idea."

"I'll call you back," he said abruptly, leaving me to wonder what exactly was going on.

I went back to chatting with Mimi, who spilled all the tea, so to speak. My girl let me know that Sanmi had come over to their apartment again. ID had planned to use the opportunity to see what Sanmi thought about me, but Sanmi started asking him about me before he had the chance. Sanmi asked if ID knew how he could connect with me. He tried to describe me to ID, since he didn't know my name. He went further to tell ID that I had been on his mind after the dinner, then he'd woken up at 6:00 the next morning with a list of questions that he believed the Lord had given him to ask me if he ever got a chance to meet me again. He'd saved these questions on his phone and shared them with ID and Mimi.

ID soon called and reiterated everything Mimi had shared, then let me know he had given Sanmi my number.

Between Mimi's messages and speaking with ID, I had no words to articulate how I felt. I dozed off on the sofa for a few minutes. By the time I opened my eyes, my phone displayed a missed call from a number I didn't have in my contacts list. I was certain it was Sanmi, but I wasn't sure whether to call him back since I was ready to sleep. I asked Mimi what she thought, and she encouraged me to call him. So, I did.

The First Call

Sanmi answered, his voice filled with energy and enthusiasm. "Yimi, what's up?" he said, as though we had either known each other forever or he was thoroughly anticipating my call. "I'm sorry for the embarrassment I caused you at your Friendsgiving dinner."

"It's nothing to worry about," I said, giggling. "I'm used to being teased like that, since I'm usually the most eligible single lady in my crew, so it was no big deal."

He let out a breath. "Good. I woke up very early the day after the dinner and had so many thoughts. I realized I'd never asked what your name was or made any effort to get your contact information. It didn't cross my mind till that morning. God told me to ask you some questions if our paths ever crossed again, so I decided to ask ID about you." He hesitated for a moment. "Actually, I wanted to go see you tomorrow morning. I don't have to catch my flight until later in the evening."

"Yeah..." I said. "ID told me. I typically have busy Mondays, so, yeah...it won't work."

"I totally understand," he said, "but I would like to ask you a couple of questions."

I sat up straighter on the sofa. "Okay."

"So," Sanmi said, "are you a Christian? If yes, why are you a Christian?

I laughed. "I don't think anyone has ever asked me that question so directly, but yes, I am. I'm a believer and follower of Christ, and pretty much everything I do in life is guided by my Christian faith. I am a Christian because I have accepted Jesus as my Lord and savior. I believe he died and rose again so I can be saved."

"Nice, nice," he said, his voice light. He sounded impressed. "That's awesome. So, what do you do in Rochester?"

I couldn't keep the sarcastic tone from my voice. "I work."

He laughed. "I meant what do you do for work?"

"I'm a project manager at Mayo Clinic," I said.

"That's right," he said, sounding sheepish. "You did share a testimony about passing your project management exam at dinner the other night. That's nice. Congrats again."

"Thank you."

"So..." he said, drawing out the word, "are you dating anyone?"

I tensed. "No, I am not dating anyone."

"May I ask why you're not dating anyone?"

"I don't believe in purposeless dating or dating for fun," I said. "I just personally don't subscribe to it." A thought struck me, and I rushed to clarify. "I'm not saying it's bad to date. I just would rather be in a relationship with the intention of getting married. I also haven't met anyone with whom I connect on that level, someone I can see the potential of marrying. Don't get me wrong, I have gone out on a few dates, had lunch and dinner here and there. I just haven't been in a committed relationship. I haven't met anyone I can commit to just yet..." I yawned.

"Wow! That is really interesting," Sanmi said, "and a totally different perspective. I love it." He paused. "I hear you yawning. I know it's late. I really would like to get to know you better. No pressure, but would you be okay with me calling you again sometime?"

"Sure, that's fine," I said. "It's honestly way past my bedtime, and I do have to be up early in the morning."

"All right. I will be flying out tomorrow evening, but I'll reach out once I'm settled in Boston." His voice deepened. "You have a good night and a great day tomorrow."

"You as well," I said. "Have a safe trip tomorrow. Good night."

"Good night."

I got up from my sofa, turned my living room lights off, and curled into my bed, thinking, *What a confident guy*. His questions were so different, so straight to the point. I sensed no judgement or intimidation at all. This, for me, was a different experience. Most of the time when I told guys what I did or where I worked, they reacted with something like, "Oh, you are a big girl" or "Oh, you're making all the money." Those reactions were often a turn-off for me.

With my eyes so heavy, I pondered the short but rather interesting conversation. My phone beeped with a text from Sanmi.

It was great speaking with you, Yimmy.
    I can't wait to know you better, 'cause I like the two things I know about you...

You take your faith seriously.
You've got a lot of positive energy and a great sense of humor.
I'll definitely keep in touch. Have a blessed week.

I turned my lights out and settled in to sleep. It wasn't at all love at first call, but this guy definitely won my interest and had my attention.

Shoot! This Guy Is My Husband!

It was a regular work Monday, but Sanmi did check in on me to see how my day was going. He mentioned that his flight got delayed but he could call me once he was settled at home. Much later that night, he called, but I had gone to bed. On Tuesday night, however, I was awake when his much awaited call came through. I excitedly answered.

Sanmi began by asking how my day had gone, shared how long his trip was, then said something very striking. During his flight, he was reading a book and couldn't help but ponder on how much faith the Wright Brothers must have had in their product to be confident enough to fly a plane.

This began the most intellectually stimulating conversation I'd ever had with a guy. We talked, laughed, and asked and answered various questions. An hour became two, then three, and it didn't feel like time had passed at all. He realized it was super late and suggested that we wrap it up, since we both had an early morning the next day.

I was swept off my feet by every word, every story, every joke, and every scripture he'd shared. It was so hard to hang up, but we eventually said our goodnights. I lay there on my sofa, clicked my phone off, and held it to my chest, looking up at the ceiling. Out of nowhere, I blurted out, "Shoot! This guy is my husband!"

I couldn't believe what I had just experienced. It was like an out of body feeling, because I had an unexplainable surety that he was "the one." I was excited and nervous and confused all at the same time. I went to bed thinking, *Wow, just like that?* It was so surreal. As I was soaking it all in, my phone beeped with a message from Sanmi.

> *I hope you are fast asleep now, 'cause I don't wanna disturb you with this...*
>
> *I just couldn't resist expressing how much I enjoyed our conversation. It really felt like thirty minutes to me. I hope you don't wake up late for work tomorrow. If you do, it wasn't me. :-)*
>
> *Have a great day at work.*

I really needed to sleep, so I didn't respond to the message, but it made me smile. I fell asleep with that smile on my face.

All Right, Lady, Come Back to Reality

As I sat in my office the following day, a lot of thoughts ran through my mind. I started thinking what I experienced the night before must have just been a fantasy, and I told myself I needed to get back to reality. I mean, come on! Was that really how people knew someone was their spouse, just because they had an interesting dialogue? This guy seemed too good to be true. While I thought all this, I grabbed a notepad and began to write a pros and cons list.

Pros	Cons
* Brilliant	~~Hug~~
* Godly	- Younger than I planned
* Familiar with the Word	talks a LOT
* Funny	Jokes a LOT
* Engaging	- style ???
* Passionate about the things of God	financial stability ???
* Educated	skinny 😕
* Seems driven	- Doesn't want kids right away.
* Very very Decent accent/ English	
* Wants to be ~~treated~~ independent	
* ~~too~~ Wonderful	
* Direct	
* Futuristic	
* Would Love to travel.	

The above is the exact list I wrote that day, and obviously the pros outweighed the cons. That didn't deter me. I continued to focus on the cons and give myself every reason why I might have gotten ahead of myself...just a little bit. I questioned what Sanmi could possibly offer me. He was slightly younger than me and just in the process of starting a more stable phase of his life. Fine, he was going to be done with his master's program soon, and that would end his internship. He still needed some time to figure his life out and fully get himself situated. Could I really hang on through all that?

These thoughts didn't stop me from responding to his texts and chatting throughout the day. His sense of humor was out of this world, his energy beamed through his text messages, and just engaging in conversation with him made my day more interesting.

We had another lengthy and enjoyable conversation that night. This made me feel a little stupid for second-guessing whether he really could be my husband. It was as though God orchestrated our conversation. Everything we spoke about made it apparent that Sanmi was a visionary with great potential. Contrary to the false words I'd been feeding my mind. Sanmi had a plan for his future. He had big dreams, and with God on his side, the sky would be just the beginning and not the limit for him.

I had meetings back-to-back at work the next day, so I didn't get a chance to see Sanmi's messages until about lunchtime, let alone reminisce about the previous night. I settled down at my desk, and the Holy Spirit suddenly prompted me to pull out my "what I want in a husband" list. I searched through my emails, then I began to read.

Tears filled my eyes. Everything I considered a pro in Sanmi was actually something I had prayed for over and over. Some of the cons were also things I had prayed for. I'd always prayed for a man with a sense of humor, who would make me laugh and never let us have a dull moment. I wanted someone who could have great conversations with me and stimulate my intellect. Yet, here I was, whining that my Sanmi talked too much.

In that moment, I realized that everything I considered a con was just an excuse to run away from facing the possibility that I had actually met a guy who checked all my boxes and might be someone I could spend the rest of my life with. God helped me see that even the somewhat vain things I complained about were fixable. Age was just a number and had no correlation with maturity. Was he skinny? I, of all people, should know it didn't take much at all for a person to put on weight. I wasn't sure what his sense of style was, since I had only seen him once, but if style was an issue and I did end up marrying him, we could easily work on that. From our conversations, I had not an ounce of doubt that his future was secure, money would never be a problem for him, and timing on having children was really all up to God.

I had to apologize to God for doubting and for trying to find everything wrong in what he had made so perfectly right. God had given me everything I had prayed for in a husband, and here I was trying to find fault in it. I felt the strong conviction that, although it had just been a matter of days, my husband had found me, God's word on that matter had now been settled in heaven, and I needed to allow things to take their natural course and manifest here on Earth.

As the weeks progressed, Sanmi would ask for us to have video calls, and I would refuse. I felt it was only right that I still kind of play hard to get. As I got comfortable, we exchanged pictures, and one Sunday evening, I succumbed to the video call request. I had just returned from a birthday party, so I had a wig on, full makeup, false eyelashes, and the whole shebang.

When I got on the video call with Sanmi, my heart melted. He was much more attractive than I remembered. I instantly loved his bright eyes, beautiful lips, and captivating smile. I shook my feelings off and told him I had a surprise for him. I set my phone down and, right before his eyes, I took off my wig, yanked out the false lashes, and I wiped off my makeup. Expecting a drastic reaction, I looked straight into the camera and said, "Nice to meet you, Sanmi."

"You look absolutely beautiful," he said, and my heart melted yet again.

Sanmi and I continued talking and getting to know each other. We had very deep conversations and asked each other about anything and everything. I mention to him that it was time for Twelve Days of Prayer and Fasting, an annual prayer festival at my church. He decided to participate in it. We fasted and prayed together.

We found ourselves talking deeper about our future, but not a future independent of one another. We shared our thoughts on marriage, as well as the type of home and size of family we wanted. We even discussed meeting each other's friends and family. Mind you, we still had only seen each other at Friendsgiving.

My Destiny Friend

As it all was happening, I hadn't shared what was going on with anyone. Doing so didn't even occur to me. Ours was already an unusual story, to say the least. One day, however, I sent a casual message to Mimi that read, "My destiny friend, I love you so much."

She replied, "I love you more."

To her, it was just a text, since it was not unlike me to express my feelings in that manner, but to me, it was a realization that our paths had not crossed by coincidence or by chance. There was a purpose on our lives and our relationship. Our destinies were aligned.

Although Mimi and her husband had not hooked Sanmi and me up, their association with him had created an avenue for us to meet. Mimi had played a pivotal role in my journey since I'd moved to the States. She had been my best friend and confidant, my go-to person. I consider her my older twin sister. She has been my one consistent friend, always loyal, forever looking out for my best interests and allowing me to learn through her life. I've never had to worry about Mimi slandering me or competing with me. My success was her success, and hers was mine.

Most people have no idea that Mimi is seven years older than me. She took interest in me when I was still a teenager and guided me. I've never had a friend whose love for me was so genuine and undiluted. Many people say I am partial towards Mimi and that I always defend her. Yes, I am, and I have many reasons why. Do we fight and get in arguments? Oh, absolutely! We don't agree on everything and sometimes step on each other's toes, but we always apologize and reach a resolution. In over fifteen years of friendship, we have never refused to speak to each other, held a grudge, or broken up. As a matter of fact, there's almost not a day when we aren't in touch, somehow. Even when one of us is away in a different country, the first thing we do is ensure that we have a line of communication.

We have gone through various storms of life together, laughed, and cried together. There were times when we wondered if we were ever gonna meet the right men and get married, times when we were not even ready to be married but focused on other areas of our lives, and times when we would agree together in prayer for our spouses. We lifted each other up and encouraged each other when we were down. Someone once told me that some friends are in your life for a reason and some just for a season. Mimi is in my life for a reason and for all my seasons.

Earlier in this book, I shared how God brought Mimi out of a horrible marriage. God gave her a second chance and, through her second chance, my own destiny was fulfilled. Her life story refired my faith in God, and when he brought her real and permanent husband into her life, I saw clearly that there was nothing God couldn't do. Her life gave me hope, and knowing ID gave me confidence that there were excellent men out there, men who fear the Lord and are able to lead and love their spouses as Christ does the church. It was almost instant that my love and respect for Mimi transmitted to ID, and it is with great joy and pride that I call him my brother.

Sorry for the break in transmission from my love story, but I had to share the importance of this friendship. Without Mimi and ID even knowing God's plan for our lives, they had slowly begun nursing the idea of connecting Sanmi and me. As I started to say, my text of love to Mimi ran deeper than its words. It touched the core of my heart when I realized that God had used my affiliation with Mimi and ID to connect me with my husband, and I cherished our relationship even more.

Mimi, ID, and I hadn't spoken about Sanmi since the day ID gave him my number. I believed they'd just done their part and moved on, and I was gradually soaking it all in.

Some weeks later, after choir practice, Mimi and I were catching up in her car as usual when she randomly asked, "The guy we gave your number to, have you guys spoken? We haven't heard anything."

I blushed and smiled from cheek to cheek.

Mimi began cheering and screamed, "Yimi, talk!"

"Sanmi is my husband," I told her. I pulled out my phone and showed her that I had saved his name as "Future Husband," unknown to him.

Extremely happy and excited, Mimi asked for every detail. We had a lengthy conversation, and she insisted that I go home with her that night so I could share the news with ID. They were the only ones who knew I had been futuristically hitched, and it was only right.

A Kiss from Heaven

Finally, Sanmi had finished his exams at school, his master's program was over, and it was time for him to come back to Minnesota. Before he met me, he was sitting on the fence about whether to leave Boston and move back to the Twin Cities after graduation. Of course, I had made his decision super easy for him.

Christmas was right around the corner, and as usual, I had made plans to spend the holidays with my friend Simi and her family in Canada. Sanmi and his friends had also made plans to go on a road trip to Texas, so he and I were both going to be away. We spoke every chance we had to be alone and exchanged messages throughout each day. I was beginning to love the idea of being in a relationship even though we hadn't made it official. We both decided to return to Minnesota the day after Christmas and, since he was to arrive hours before I did, agreed that he would connect with Mimi to get my car and pick me up from the airport.

The day finally arrived, and I was excited to be heading home —even more excited to see Sanmi. Once I landed, I called him to let him know I had arrived. He was already waiting for me. My heart raced a bit as I walked out. He got out of the car and gave me the warmest hug ever. I couldn't stop smiling, filled with a feeling I had never experienced. He put my bags in the trunk, and we headed to Rochester. I can't recall precisely what we spoke about, but there was not a moment of silence for the entire hour of our drive.

In a previous conversation, Sanmi had said Texas Roadhouse was his favorite restaurant, so I told him we had one in Rochester about five minutes from my apartment. We stopped at the restaurant, and we considered it our first date.

Sanmi complimented me from time to time, saying things like, "You're so cute" or "Your hairstyle really suits you" and "I love your smile." He cracked me up so much over dinner, and we had a great time. I was definitely going on another date with this guy!

When we got to my apartment, I put my things away, showed Sanmi around, and got settled in.

He sat on the sofa and pulled me down to sit on his lap. He held me really close and said he was so happy to be with me. At last, he blurted out the words my heart had been yearning for. "I love you so much," he said. "I really wanted to tell you in person, not over the phone. I loved you over the phone, but I love you so much more in person." He planted the softest, most passionate kiss on my lips, a kiss from heaven.

It had been a little over ten years since I had shared a kiss with anyone, and at that moment, I felt it was worth the wait. Sanmi was very respectful of me, and we were in agreement on waiting till we were married before having sex.

Reflection and Prayer

Write down the names of some people (friends, family, colleagues, pastors, etc.) God has put in your life who have propelled you to achieve great things or added value to your life.

Thank you, Lord, for: ____.

CHAPTER 9

GOD PUT A YES ON MY LIFE

At this point, I know it all must seem too good to be true. The same thought ran through my mind daily. Many times, I would find myself in deep thought and blurt out, "Just like that!" Step by step, God took me back to a place of remembrance. It had been almost two years since the Hallelujah Challenge where we had declared that we received miracles that would happen "just like that." My just-like-that miracle didn't happen the week of the challenge, that month, or even that year. It waited almost two years, but when it did happen, it was "just like that."

It also dawned on me that Sanmi and I crossed paths exactly seven days after the Thirty-Six Hours of Praise festival at my church. I had gone to that Praise Festival with a list of prayer requests, and all those requests were for family members and friends, prayers for everyone I held dear. That year, I had just one request for myself, my standard prayer for a husband. I remain in awe of God, as he is, indeed, an on-time God.

He has made everything beautiful in its time. He has also set eternity in the human heart; yet no one can fathom what God has done from beginning to end.

— ECCLESIASTES 3:11 (NIV)

Every day began to feel dreamy. It seemed like I was in a trance. I became more joyful, and I started to feel and look more beautiful. I suddenly started getting more compliments. I was more productive at work. There was a calmness in my heart and in my spirit. Although Sanmi hadn't asked me to be his wife, deep down in my heart, I knew he was the husband for me, and I was sure God would confirm the same thing to him. I believed God had done the ultimate thing in my life, and he had done it "just like that," when I least expected. I finally was able to check off the number one item that showed up on every prayer list I had ever written. My ultimate prayer request had now become my ultimate testimony and praise report. I began to live and experience the word of God in Psalm 126 (KJV):

> *When the Lord turned again the captivity of Zion, we were like them that dream.*
>
> *Then was our mouth filled with laughter, and our tongue with singing: then said they among the heathen, The Lord hath done great things for them.*
>
> *The Lord hath done great things for us; whereof we are glad.*
>
> *Turn again our captivity, O Lord, as the streams in the south.*
>
> *They that sow in tears shall reap in joy.*
>
> *He that goeth forth and weepeth, hearing precious seed, shall doubtless come again with rejoicing, bringing his sheaves with him.*

It had now been about two months since Sanmi and I started talking and getting to know each other. We spent as much time as we could together, talked for hours, and had a lot of fun together. As we learned more about each other, we fell more in love. Of course, being the planner that I am, I started to mentally map out our future. I would perhaps get to know him for a couple more months, then we could work on meeting each other's family and friends. Sanmi was job-hunting, now that he had relocated to Minnesota, and he would need some time to find his rhythm, get settled in his job—once he got one—and overall be more comfortable and independent in Minnesota. He probably wouldn't propose to me until the end of the year, and we could get married the following year, 2020. With this plan, I didn't need to rush or bring unnecessary attention to the relationship, so I continued to enjoy courting my one-and-done partner.

Sanmi lived in the Twin Cities with his older sister and her family, while I was still in Rochester. Sometimes, he would drive up to visit me during the week or come pick me up on Friday to go to the Cities, so we mostly spent time together over the weekends.

On one particular weekend, I had driven myself to the Cities and was at church that Sunday. We had just finished praise and worship, and prayer commenced. I opened my eyes after prayers and couldn't believe who I was looking at. Sanmi stood right there in the congregation. He hadn't told me he would be coming, so I was totally surprised, nervous, and excited all at the same time. I wasn't ready to be seen with him, so I wasn't sure how to react. He came out as a first-time visitor, and I tried not to make eye contact but couldn't ignore how handsome he looked and how he smiled from cheek to cheek. I snuck out of church to avoid speaking with him in the auditorium, then I snuck up on him outside. He didn't understand my reasoning for the hide-and-seek game I was playing, and to be honest, I didn't either. I guess I was just nervous and really wasn't used to being in the spotlight like I would if people found out I was in a relationship.

We decided to pick up lunch and go hang out at Mimi and ID's apartment. They were going to be out that afternoon, but they'd said we could stay there while they were gone so we could spend time together before I had to drive back to Rochester.

We ate our lunch and shared our insights from the message

we'd heard at church. One conversation led to another and another, until Sanmi pulled me close on the couch where we sat and asked a question I absolutely did not see coming.

"Are you willing to start from ground zero with me?" he asked. "If you would have me, I want to spend the rest of my life with you. Will you marry me?"

I was startled for a second, because I definitely didn't think Sanmi would be ready to marry me two months into our courtship. Here I was, in his arms and, with all the peace in my heart, I said, "I will start from ground zero with you." I laughed, trying to remain composed. "Yes, I will marry you."

This was a clear agreement that our courtship was officially leading to the altar. Sanmi then shared his favorite scripture. "But the path of the just is as the shining light, that shineth more and more unto the perfect day" (Proverbs 4:18 KJV). He expressed his confidence that we could only get better and better with God on our side, and I believed him with everything inside me.

The moment was so surreal. I had thought, yet again, that I had my...*our* future all planned out, but God's ways are not my ways, neither are his thoughts my thoughts. I drove back to Rochester with a whole new realization. I would be getting married sooner than I'd anticipated. So, now that we knew we wanted to be married, what was next? How did we prepare ourselves for this? And the questions kept flowing through my mind on my long drive home.

Introductions

Weeks went by, and Sanmi and I had conversations about informing our parents and family members that we were courting and had plans to get married. We knew this would be a lot to take in, so we decided to inform our families of our relationship and leave it at that.

First, I told my brother. He wasn't surprised that I was seeing someone, as every weekend I stayed with him, I either stayed out late or was on the phone all night with someone. He really had a blast teasing me about having a boyfriend. He'd say, "Aw!" at everything I said and called it all *cute*. Next, I told my mom, and she immediately had a number of questions to ask. She was extremely excited and said she had butterflies in her belly. I could tell she was on the other side of the phone blushing and smiling from cheek to cheek. I was certain that she would drop the call and tell my grandmother everything I had shared. Since that went well, I began to tell my friends, one by one, about Sanmi, and everyone was excited for me. Many people said that I had never spoken about any guy the way I talked about Sanmi, so it had to be really serious.

Sanmi had told all his friends about me, so he just needed to inform his family. He told his older sister first and said her first response was, "Your pupils were dilated as you spoke. You must be in love." Not a shocking response, since she's a medical doctor, but I couldn't hold back the laughter when he shared that. He said she was eager to meet me.

My first meeting with his family was quite unexpected. Sanmi and I had gone out on an adventure. He took me on my first virtual reality ride, FlyOver America. It uses special effects to simulate flight over landmarks and scenic landscapes. I hadn't even known about it and was amazed. That ranked as one of our best dates at the time. We had dinner, then drove to his place so I could drop him off. It was late at night, so we figured it was safe to assume that his family had gone to bed. We sat in the car in the driveway and got carried away talking. After about an hour, the garage doors opened, and we both looked around in total shock. The family had also been out and had just returned. I had no route of escape. I just said *hello* while still sitting in the car, but Kemi, Sanmi's older sister, summoned me to come inside. And there it was, my first unplanned introduction to his family.

I met his sister and her husband, Kayode; his dad; and

Kayode's dad. I also got to meet his wonderful nieces—Ini, Abigail, and Dami—whom I had actually met virtually. They were all so warm and lovely to me. They offered me all types of appetizers and soft drinks and told me to feel comfortable, as this was now also my home. We talked briefly, then I said I needed to head home since it was so late. Sister Kemi said she would love to host me properly and she would coordinate with Sanmi on the best time to do so. I loved the family already. They were even more lovely than I had imagined.

As time went by, we began more official meetings, starting with Sanmi meeting my older brother, Lasun, and my cousin Funsho and his family. They joked that he needed to know I had *two* big brothers who would handle him if he dared misbehave. He blended right in, and I loved how awesome and playful he was with my nieces, Ella and Gabby. My brother and cousin also loved him right off the bat!

Next, I introduced him to my three uncles and their families. I anticipated this being very dramatic and, I tell you, it was...in a good way. My uncles, their wives, my brother, and some of my cousins had gathered at my oldest uncle's house that Sunday afternoon. Sanmi and I went to join them after church. My aunties broke out in singing and dancing the instant we walked in. As anyone from our culture would, they assumed that we intended to marry because I'd never brought a guy over to meet the family.

Sanmi smiled from cheek to cheek, but I wanted the floor to open up and swallow me. Finally, my aunties stopped and said, "Iremide has come. We've waited so many years to meet you." I grinned at their use of the name I'd called my imagined future husband—which, you may recall, means "my goodness has come." Then, the aunties started singing a Yoruba song that translated to "Welcome, my goodness. Welcome, my goodness of joy. Welcome, my goodness has come in." It was quite the most epic and dramatic introduction I've had to make in my entire life. Everyone interacted with Sanmi and gave him a warm welcome.

Later on, Sister Kemi invited me over. Boy, I had never been hosted by anyone like that! She had cooked up a storm and set a beautiful table. The entire family sat down for lunch, and I felt so comfortable, accepted, and genuinely loved. They asked a number of questions just to get to know me better. Sanmi's family was a lot cooler and calmer than mine had been, so I didn't have any dramatic or embarrassing moments.

Sanmi's Dad really engaged me in conversation, interested in my faith, where I worshiped, what I did for work, and the like. He stimulated my intellect, and I could see a lot of similarities between him and Sanmi. It melted my heart when Sister Kemi said she was happy to have me as a sister, considering she is the only girl out of six siblings.

Sanmi's family embodied the type that I had always hoped and prayed to marry into. A wonderful Christian family where it is apparent that love dwells. When it was time for me to leave and begin my journey back to Rochester, Sister Kemi packed me a variety of meals, snacks, and drinks that could last me for days. She ranks as one of the most wonderful individuals I have ever met, and I was glad to have her as a sister as well.

Finally, I needed to officially introduce Sanmi to my friends. Most of my close friends attend my church, so on the few occasions Sanmi visited our church, he got a chance to interact with Tosin and Tope. Nothing formal had occurred, but by this time, everyone in my circle pretty much knew who he was and was well aware that I was in a relationship.

One evening, I was chatting with Tope and mentioned that I couldn't believe it had been three months since Sanmi and I had been in a relationship. She said she was also surprised at how fast time had gone by. She said everyone would appreciate it if I formally introduced Sanmi to my friends and let them have a chance to get to know him. I was happy to hear that, as I had been waiting for them to express interest in getting to know him. So, I told her I would check Sanmi's availability, and we could decide on a day.

We picked a Friday night to hang out, date night with Sanmi, Tope, Sayo, and me. I was looking forward to this because it had been a while since the girls and I got to kick back. About a week before the set date, Tope said we had to cancel because she had to run some errands with her mom. This seemed really unlike Tope. I had a number of questions, but I decided I'd let it go and plan to reschedule for a different time.

Something Is Cooking

Right after our first conversation about getting married, Sanmi would lead me to a jewelry store any time we went to a shopping mall, and he'd ask what types of rings I liked. I'd give the selections a quick glance, then let him know I didn't see anything I particularly loved. I eventually showed him a picture of a ring I had saved on my phone. I'd carried the picture of that ring for about seven years, hoping I would someday have one just like it. When he saw the picture, his eyes widened.

"Don't freak out," I said. "The picture just depicts the style I would like. Whatever ring you decide to get me, even if it's plastic, I will love and appreciate it."

I guess Sanmi continued to deliberate on the image I had shown him, because one Saturday, he brought me into an actual ring shop that specialized in engagement and wedding rings. Our eyes locked, and we giggled as the jeweler showed us many beautiful rings. I decided to show her my ring picture. Our jaws dropped when she said the store had that exact ring. Considering how old that picture was, I hadn't thought I would find the exact ring, but I would have been happy with something similar in style. I grew teary when I saw the ring. It was even more beautiful than the picture. There it was, my dream ring, on my finger.

After all the oohing, aahing, and tearing, Sanmi asked how

much the ring cost. Let's just say, I suddenly didn't love the ring as much anymore. Okay, maybe I exaggerated a bit. I still loved the ring, but the price? It was not as beautiful. I didn't want to look at anything else. I was kind of done ring shopping for that day, because the probability of having my dream ring was slim.

After a while, I began doing more research on this dream ring. I thought it was a victory that we at least found it at a shop. That meant, if I looked farther and harder, I could find it somewhere else. I was not wrong. An old friend told me about the jewelry store where he had gotten his wife's engagement ring, and Sanmi and I decided to make inquiries. We discovered that we could get the ring there, but the price still wasn't pretty. After this, Sanmi basically commanded me to end my research on the ring and just let him figure it out.

I feared my choice of a ring might have run him to the wall, because thereafter he shut down any conversations about it. He became so nonchalant and dismissive when the ring subject came up. I consoled myself by thinking he had already proposed to me without a ring, so him buying one was just a formality. I loved him, and I would be happy with whatever ring he gave me, even if it wasn't this dream ring of mine.

My dear Tosin, who loves photos just as much as I do—actually, much more than I do—told me she and her husband had come across a beautiful apartment complex that would be great for pictures. Her husband, Moyo, is a professional photographer, so he's always on the lookout for great photography locations for his clients.

"We have the spot, A Mill Artist Lofts, booked to do a photoshoot for our daughters," Tosin said. "It would be nice if you and Sanmi come along and get some pictures, too."

"You know Yimi never turns down an opportunity to take pictures!" I said. "I'm all the way on board. It has been four months since Sanmi and I started courting, and most of our pictures are selfies, so I'm really excited to get some professional pictures."

"Don't worry," she said. "You can take several shots, change your outfits, and just make it a fun photo session."

I told Sanmi what Tosin had suggested, and he was okay with the idea but not half as excited as I was. About a week before the photoshoot—around the time Tope cancelled our plans for Sanmi and me to hang out with her and Sayo—Tosin suggested having other couples join in the shoot as well. So, once they were done with the kid's photoshoot, the adults could take advantage of the location to get some beautiful shots. A brilliant idea! I told Mimi to come with ID, since it was sounding like a couples thing. I'd already begun envisioning the wonderful pictures we could get and was super excited.

Sanmi's energy level for this photoshoot was almost non-existent. I tried to persuade him that it would be fun. I just needed him to be half as excited as I was, but I couldn't seem to get his energy up. This made me begin to lose excitement, but Tosin's energy was contagious.

She asked what I planned to wear, and I went on about my sweaters, jeans, and sandals. Tosin was not having it. She said I needed to treat it like a test run for my future engagement shoot. She shared several inspiration shots with me, and we spent time playing dress-up and picking my outfits via facetime. I showed them to Sanmi so he could coordinate his outfits with mine, and he assured me he would see what he had that would work.

Finally, the weekend arrived, and on Friday, I was all packed for my trip to the Twin Cities. In addition to the photoshoot on Saturday, a surprise birthday lunch was being planned for one of my aunties in church, so it was going to be a fun and eventful weekend. I was catching up with Titi, another friend who's like a big sister, and she asked what my plans were for the weekend. I told her about the couples' photoshoot with friends and the surprise birthday lunch. I mentioned that I wasn't sure whether to get my makeup done professionally for the photoshoot, and Titi could not fathom that I didn't already have a makeup appointment scheduled. She said that should be a no-brainer and even offered to pay for the makeup. She told me to call to schedule an appointment with the makeup artist immediately to ensure that she had an opening for the next day, since this was so last-minute. She kicked me off the phone, and I called to schedule an appointment.

And Just Like That, I Am Rocking!

As usual for a Friday night, Sanmi and I met up for a date, since we weren't going to hang out with Tope and Sayo. Sanmi suggested that we go to a restaurant to just chat and have appetizers, because it was quite late. We went to a sushi bar I recommended and had a really chill evening. I was a little surprised Sanmi was okay with us going there, since he is not a huge fan of seafood and absolutely dislikes fish. He was so loving, made me laugh so hard, and continued to express his love for me. He had surprised me by getting his hair cut for the photoshoot. I was relieved that he showed some enthusiasm.

The morning of our photoshoot, I went to Mimi's new house. I noticed she had gotten her nails done, which made me realize that mine were unusually messed up, so I decided to go get them done before my makeup appointment. Since I was unsure of what Sanmi planned to wear, I also stopped at the store to pick up a few things for him before I went over to meet up with him.

Finally, he was a lot more enthused about the photoshoot! We took selfies in the car on our ride to the location. It seemed like we were the last ones to get there. Ify and Kenyeh were already taking pictures when we arrived. The building was really beautiful and artistic.

I wanted to see Tosin's daughters, Tessy and Love, in their costumes for their pictures, but Tosin urged me to put on my first outfit so Sanmi and I could take some pictures in that part of the building before going to the room where the girls were having their shoot. She coordinated our poses, and we took great pictures. We also took some group pictures with Mimi and ID, then it was time for a change of clothing. The group focused a lot of attention on Sanmi and me, and I kept thinking how sweet Tosin was, going over and beyond as though we were celebrating something. These were supposed to be pictures for the fun of it, but the shoot was being professionally executed.

We changed into our second outfits and took pictures at another beautiful part of the building. I was beginning to get tired, but I suddenly realized the part of the building we were in would be great for engagement pictures. I asked Mimi to let me wear her ring for some of our shots. I was curious to see what Sanmi and I would look like taking real engagement pictures, just for the fun of it.

I was getting more tired and cranky. Sanmi was chewing gum, and the sound felt like it was piercing my brain. I was hungry, too, but we still had to make our final change of outfits for the last set of pictures. Our shoot director, Tosin, said she could sense my tiredness, so she had us wrap things up on that set, and we went to change into the final outfits.

While I got ready, she asked Sanmi and Ify to go with Moyo to scout for a good location for our final pictures. Moyo said he had a few options in mind, but he would like to get their opinion, so the boys left. I stayed with the ladies to freshen my makeup, swap out my wig, and change my dress.

Tosin got a call, informing her that the guys had found a spot and we needed to head down. As we began walking, I handed Mimi back her ring. We cracked jokes as we took phone pictures on the way. My toes were burning because I was wearing heels, and I whined, asking why the guys had to go so far to find a spot for a picture. I walked as though my legs were bowed and asked Mimi if she would still be my friend if I had bowlegs. Tosin, Kenyeh, and Mimi all laughed.

We were still laughing when I noticed rose petals on the floor leading into a room. Moyo held a video camera, and loads of other cameras started flashing. I turned back in shock and found Mimi, Tosin, and Kenyeh holding their phones and recording me. In the room, all my close friends had gathered, along with my brother and cousin. I held my heart and called out uncontrollably, "Jesus! Jesus! Jesus!" All I could say was *Jesus* as everyone urged me to go into the room.

My heart stopped and my eyes widened when I spotted my Sanmi—on one knee in the center of a bed of red rose petals arranged in the shape of a heart, with candles all around, and holding a bouquet of red roses. Balloons and lighted candles were scattered everywhere, and my favorite love songs were playing in the background. I had never imagined what it would look or feel like when my future husband proposed to me. I had totally skipped that in my planning phase, but that moment was heaven on Earth. There was not a thing I would have added or subtracted. It was subtle compared with some I'd seen on the internet, it was classy, it was elegant, and everything was perfect.

Still on one knee and with the biggest smile on his face, Sanmi handed me the bouquet of red roses and took my other hand. "I love you so much," he said. "I wish I was Shakespeare for this moment, but all I can say is, I love you so much and I want to spend the rest of my life with you. Olayimika Modupeola Olagboye-Coker"—he pulled out a little ring box— "will you marry me?"

"Of course I'll marry you," I said. Then, he opened the ring box, and I screamed my lungs out. Again, I yelled, "Jesus!"

Sanmi had bought my dream ring, the exact ring I had carried around as a picture in my phone. Again, Sanmi had made my dream come true. It was the biggest surprise of my life. I was swept off my feet, and I hugged him, kissed him, and couldn't stop saying, "Thank you! Thank you! Thank you!"

This moment marked the beginning of the happiest days of my entire life. I couldn't think of any day or occasion prior to this when I have honestly felt the pure, true, genuine joy and happiness that I felt right then. I sang. I danced. I went on my knees and thanked God with no shame, for honoring me and answering my prayers even beyond what I had asked. My heart was filled with so much gratitude to God. He put a big "Yes!" on my life and a beautiful rock on my finger, and I absolutely loved it!

I later discovered that my close friends all over the world had witnessed this moment virtually. Simi had joined in from Canada, Jumoke all the way from Nigeria, and the biggest shocker was Dolapo from London, with whom I had spoken earlier in the day. She had given me not a clue.

All the puzzle pieces now fit. Tope had asked me on two occasions what my plans were for the weekend since we couldn't get together. On Friday, I'd told her I had a photoshoot with Tosin and a surprise birthday party, so I'd wondered why she asked again Saturday morning. All of Sanmi's nonchalance about the ring or the photoshoot had been a cover so he wouldn't give away the surprise. It made sense, now, why Titi insisted I get my makeup done. Thank God for the Holy Spirit, who opened my eyes to see Mimi's pretty nails and prompted me to do mine.

Finally, the chief master planner, set director, and proposal project manager, Tosin, my exceptional gift from God. She'd helped me put my outfit together and started conversations to find out what I thought an ideal proposal would look like, while I had no clue it was mine we discussed. I later found out that Sanmi had told Tope of his intention to propose, and that's why she'd cancelled our plans for the girls to hang out with Sanmi so abruptly. Everything was perfectly executed, no clues were given, and I was thoroughly surprised.

Sanmi and I took many pictures, some with our friends and family present. I took pictures with the cutest engagement cake, which Sayo had bought, and we all went to a Thai restaurant to celebrate the engagement. I got so many calls and texts on our way to the restaurant, as my friends had begun posting pictures and videos on social media. My mom called to congratulate us, her voice beaming with so much joy. I was so thankful to all my friends for planning the best and most beautiful proposal I had ever witnessed.

That night, I got on my knees and thanked Sanmi again. He broke the bank, gave his heart, and gave his all to ensure that I was the happiest girl in the world. I am, to this day, still thankful for what he did.

Reflection and Prayer

Write down some things that God has done to gladden your heart and give you genuine joy and happiness—things you didn't ask him for.

Father, I thank you for: ___.

CHAPTER 10

A REASON AND A SEASON

I hope you have enjoyed my fairytale journey to finding true love God's way and that it was as soothing to you as it was to me. It is a beautiful testament to what only God can do. Everything God has a hand in turns out not just good, but excellent, beyond human comprehension.

> *Now to him who is able to do immeasurably more than all we ask or imagine, according to his power that is at work within us.*

> — EPHESIANS 3:20 (NIV)

As you can see from the stories I've shared, all that I had asked and looked to God for in the area of marriage began to manifest before my eyes. As I approached each phase, it grew clearer and clearer that God had ordained my union with Sanmi. We became living testimonies of Sanmi's favorite quote that "We can only get better."

Be Careful What You Pray For

As we have learned so far, we can trust God for anything at

all. Nothing is too hard for him to do. We only need to trust him and his timing, and when he fulfills what we've asked, it will indeed be marvelous in our eyes. Jeremiah 32:17 says, "Ah, Sovereign LORD, you have made the heavens and the earth by your great power and outstretched arm. Nothing is too hard for you" (NIV). The sad truth is, when God does these things that you have been trusting him for, many will rejoice with you, but not everyone will truly be happy for you.

About three days after my engagement, a close friend—who I will refer to as Sara—called me to express some of her feelings about me and my engagement. She said she felt I was being secretive about my relationship, and it was not right that I hadn't brought Sanmi around my friends. She also said that I generally would do things and not tell her about them. For instance, I would travel on vacation and not share the names of the friends I was travelling with. From all she said, it was apparent that she and another supposedly close friend—whom I will call Betty—had discussed and agreed on this.

My heart broke. I didn't understand where her thoughts and feelings were coming from, because she had flown down from a trip to attend my engagement. She'd made the most heartfelt post of all on social media, expressing her happiness for me and emphasizing how much I deserved what had come my way. We had spoken the day after the engagement, and I'd believed she was sharing in my joy.

During that call, through my pain, I listened, astonished. After she had expressed her feelings, I reminded Sara that, on my second official date ever with Sanmi, we had run into her and her boyfriend at the movie theatre and I had introduced them. I'd called her later the same night to let her know I had only recently met him and was waiting to see where things would go. I pointed out that this was a call I didn't have to make and an explanation I didn't have to give, especially if I truly had something to hide.

Shortly after Sanmi had first expressed his intention to marry me, I had called Sara to update her on how things were going between Sanmi and me. I told her how certain I was that he was my husband and that we would probably get married towards the end of the year. She and I had spoken at length that Saturday, which made it even the more surprising that she now claimed I tried to hide things from her.

I apologized to her, because I honestly didn't know what else to say or do. I truly believed I had done my best to keep her involved, but apparently, I hadn't done enough. I told her that, had Sanmi not proposed to me when he did, she probably wouldn't feel this way, and she agreed with me. When she realized how hurt I was, she apologized and said she didn't intend to make me cry. She just wanted me to know how she felt.

I was hurt to the bone marrow and couldn't believe that the friends I loved so much—friends I constantly prayed for and had prayed with as we all trusted God for a spouse—found fault in me or in what God had done for me. I cried bitterly at work, to the point that some of my co-workers thought my three-day old engagement was broken. It hurt that I was left to question the genuineness of the happiness Sara and Betty had expressed at my engagement. It was disappointing that, at this time when I was beaming and basking in the joy of being engaged to the love of my life, a friend had dampened my spirit.

All through that day, my conversation with Sara continued to replay in my head. How could she and Betty be so upset with me, especially when God had just answered my prayer after so many years?

That night, I cried and let my feelings out to God. He reminded me of a prayer I had prayed repeatedly: "God, give me an enviable testimony." I grabbed my prayer journal and, as I flipped through the pages, spotted the prayer requests I had written, asking for an enviable testimony, but I'd never asked him for the grace or the wisdom to cope with the answer to this prayer. What a revelation! I didn't feel as bad anymore, because I realized I had gotten what I'd asked for—not how I'd imagined it, but I learned a great lesson that night. Be careful what you pray for.

After this, things became awkward between Sara and me, and we grew farther and farther apart. As months passed, we made a number of attempts to rectify things, but nothing seemed to work. She continued to imply that she and Betty felt the same way.

I struggled to cope with the fact that these friends who I believed had become my sisters were growing so distant from me at this crucial time in my life. I'd believed we would be girlfriends for life, regardless of our disagreements and differences. I had envisioned our spouses and kids being friends, and I couldn't figure out the reason why all that had changed. I'd imagined that, at this exciting point in my life, they would share in my joy and go through the journey with me, considering we had shared so many hurts, heartbreaks, and disappointments. Why now? They knew my story. I had never been as lucky as most people in this aspect of my life, so why had I suddenly become the enemy?

I tried to make things right. I apologized, regardless of who was wrong, but Sara seemed to perceive every attempt negatively or interpret it wrongly, and I started to feel like a nuisance. After all, it takes two to weather any storm in friendship. Though we are all imperfect, I thought we could settle our differences amicably, but nothing seemed to change in our relationship.

Although I was very hurt and upset, I decided to speak with Betty about this situation, since I had begun feeling a dislike towards her and Sara. I'll be honest, reaching out to her was a real test of my faith and one of the most difficult things I'd ever had to do, but God continued to remind me of what his word says on such things. "If it is possible, as far as it depends on you, live at peace with everyone." (Romans 12:18 NIV.)

I paid Betty a surprise visit early on a Sunday morning and

attended service with her. The message in that service was another confirmation that God was ordering my footsteps and that, regardless of how wronged I felt, I needed to do right by maintaining peace. After the service, we went back to Betty's house, and I expressed how displeased I was that she and Sara had been having conversations about me and believed I didn't involve them enough in my relationship with Sanmi. I told her this was even worse because they expressed these feelings right after I got engaged.

Betty apologized and seemed sincere. She said, "I honestly understand how you feel, and if I were in your shoes, I would feel the same way." She explained that Sara had shared her thoughts on this, but that she, Betty, had only acted as a sounding board for Sara. I told her my trust was broken and, even when Sara had extended a positive gesture, I'd really questioned her motives. We had a lengthy conversation, and though it was very difficult, I was able to bring myself to truly forgive them both.

Things have since not been the same between Sara and me, though we remain at peace and cordial with each other. We support each other when needed, check in on each other, and interact well when we see each other. We do not share the depth and intimacy that friends share, though.

Pastor Sola Olowokere once preached a message on relationships. In it, he said, "You know you have a close relationship with a person if you share your challenges, joys, plans, and weaknesses with one another." Sara and I once had that kind of relationship. I now fully understand the saying that, "some friends are in your life for a reason and some for a season."

Betty and I have remained friends. She hasn't fully earned my trust again, but we have continued to relate well. I love both Betty and Sara dearly, and I continue to pray for them, support them, and wish them well, as I do everyone around me.

Although I was hesitant, the Holy Spirit impressed on my

heart how important it was that I share this aspect of my journey. We ought to be aware and vigilant because, as God is in the business of beautifying our lives and bringing us joy, the enemy cannot handle this. He will come in any way, shape, or form to obstruct our peace. This obstruction could come in the form of friends, as it did in my case. It could be family members, like Joseph's in the Bible. His brothers plotted to kill him because he was full of wisdom, loved, and favored by their father (see Genesis 37). His brothers were horrible to him, but he persevered, and God gave him victory over them (see Genesis 50).

There is great benefit in genuinely celebrating and rejoicing with those who celebrate. As I had shared previously, during my time of waiting I was very intentional about rejoicing and celebrating with those who were getting married. I sowed seeds, giving my time to help them in any capacity I could, because I desired to be blessed in that area as well. Actions speak louder than words, so in addition to saying congratulations, we should make sure our actions and demeanor show that we truly mean what we have said and expect nothing in return. I have a personal saying: "It isn't always *where* you sow that you reap, but it is *what* you sow that you reap." Therefore, always sow love and kindness. God, who is the ultimate rewarder, sees all, and according to Romans 2:6, "he will repay everyone according to what that person has done" (ISV).

As you approach your promised land—become a spouse or parent, get a new job, move to a new city, start a new business, buy a new home, or receive whatever you're praying for—be prepared to leave some relationships behind. Not all friendships are meant to last forever. It is very hurtful to let go, but real-life situations expose who truly wants to see you win. Not everyone riding with you is riding *for* you, and as you begin to manifest your life's purpose and reach your life's dreams, it will become more apparent who truly is for you.

Lastly, our Lord and savior Jesus Christ, who is almighty, also experienced rejection. He fully understands what pain and rejection feel like, since one of his followers who broke bread with him ended up turning him in to the enemy to be killed (see Matthew 26:14-16). The psalmist David also wrote in Psalms 41:9, "Even my close friend, someone I trusted, one who shared my bread, has turned against me" (NIV). This shows that we are not alone.

Being hurt by those we love might be inevitable, but we should remain fervent in prayer and respond in love, trusting God to help us through our healing process and bring those who have hurt us to repentance. As you trust God for your miracle, whatever it may be, if you keep your faith and gaze on God, your answers will surely come. If, like me, you have asked God for enviable miracles, that is certainly okay. There are no restrictions on God's abilities, but please remember to ask for the grace and wisdom to receive and handle your miracle.

Love in Action

Love must be sincere. Hate what is evil; cling to what is good. Be devoted to one another in love. Honor one another above yourselves. Never be lacking in zeal, but keep your spiritual fervor, serving the Lord. Be joyful in hope, patient in affliction, faithful in prayer. Share with the Lord's people who are in need. Practice hospitality.

Bless those who persecute you; bless and do not curse. Rejoice with those who rejoice; mourn with those who mourn. Live in harmony with one another. Do not be proud, but be willing to associate with people of low position. Do not be conceited.

Do not repay anyone evil for evil. Be careful to do what is right in the eyes of everyone. If it is possible, as far as it depends on you, live at peace with everyone. Do not take revenge, my dear friends, but leave room for God's wrath, for it is written: "It is mine to avenge; I will repay," says the Lord. On the contrary:

"If your enemy is hungry, feed him; if he is thirsty, give him

something to drink. In doing this, you will heap burning coals on his head."

Do not be overcome by evil, but overcome evil with good.

— ROMANS 12:9-21 (NIV)

Let us not become weary in doing good, for at the proper time we will reap a harvest if we do not give up.

— GALATIANS 6:9 (NIV)

Reflection and Prayer

Write down the names of some people who have hurt or disappointed you. List your hurts, then ask God to heal you and help you completely forgive them and to give you grace to love them like Christ would. Start by thanking God for them and the good times you have shared.

CHAPTER 11

LINES ARE FALLING IN
PLEASANT PLACES

According to Psalms 37:23, "The steps of a good man are ordered by the LORD: and he delighteth in his way" (KJV). Sanmi and I began to enjoy God's divine direction as we transitioned to being Fiancé and Fiancée. As I tried to get used to the title, I was always shy when teased about being a bride-to-be, but I was also excited. Our engagement was now as official as it could be.

Sanmi and I continued to learn about each other and grow together. About a month after he proposed, he secured a good job in the Twin Cities. It was a very well-paying job, but wasn't in the domain in which he wanted to foster his career. We agreed that he should take the job, as it was better than not working, and as time went on, he would continue to explore opportunities in his areas of expertise. Things were very quickly taking shape for Sanmi, and he was becoming more financially stable. I would often quote this scripture to him: "The boundary lines have fallen for (you) in pleasant places; surely (you) have a delightful inheritance" (Psalm 16:6 NIV).

We began planning our lives and future together with more depth, intentionality, and action. We also began exploring options for our wedding date. We agreed that we wanted a small intimate wedding, with our close friends and family members present and keeping the number of attendees minimal.

Since we are both of Nigerian descent—from Yoruba, which is in the western part of Nigeria—we had to factor in the traditional ceremonies. Those begin with a formal family introduction, in which the members of the groom's family come bearing gifts to be formally introduced to the bride's family. To the bride's parents, the groom expresses his intention to marry their daughter, and the bride's family gives a response. If it is a positive response, they give a return gift to the groom's family, showing that they are in support of their children marrying each other. Next, the traditional wedding precedes the white or church wedding, which typically takes place a day or two later.

Our first step was to coordinate with our families on when to have the family introduction. As we made plans to do so, Sanmi and I also prayerfully considered possible wedding dates.

One day, Sanmi said, "If November 23, 2019 is a Saturday, we should get married that day."

Lo and behold, it was a Saturday, exactly a year from the day we met. I loved the idea, but wondered how we could space things out to include both a traditional wedding ceremony and a church wedding ceremony.

I reminded Sanmi that, although I wanted a small and intimate wedding, I also wanted an opportunity for my mom to be celebrated. She had dreamed of me getting married for as long as I could remember, and for all she had done for me—despite being a single parent all my life—I wanted her to be honored. If we had our wedding in the States, my mom might end up seeming like a guest, as most of her friends and social counterparts were in Nigeria. I said that having our wedding in Nigeria would allow my dream of honoring my mom to come true, but our desire for a small intimate wedding might be far-fetched.

Sanmi agreed to having the wedding in Nigeria, since most of his siblings, his grandma, and other close family members lived in Nigeria as well. We agreed that our traditional wedding ceremony could be a bit elaborate, giving our parents the opportunity to invite all their friends and loved ones to celebrate with them, but we would remain firm on keeping our church wedding as intimate as possible. We decided to have this on a weekday, to help with curbing the number of attendees. We chose November 28, 2019, which happened to fall right on Thanksgiving Day in the US that year.

We were both very happy with our decision and felt it was divinely orchestrated by the Lord. Sanmi's birthday is September 23, mine is December 23, we met on November 23, and now we'd be getting married traditionally on November 23.

Although we felt great about the dates we had picked, I was a little nervous because my cousin Miriam was getting married in May of the same year. Hers was a destination wedding in London and Malta, a huge but planned expense for the family, since we'd had over a year's notice to prepare. I wondered how my family would react to the fact that I was planning to get married the same year and it was also going to be a wedding outside the US. I prayed about it, and God continued to give me peace over it, so my worries began to subside.

I called my mom first to share the dates with her. To my greatest surprise, the first thing she said was that she'd also gotten married on November 28, in 1981. I found that a huge coincidence. She had no concerns with the dates and encouraged us to begin committing both days to God in prayer.

Sanmi and I shared our wedding dates with the rest of our family members, and their excitement and support overwhelmed us. Although it would be a big expense, our families did not express any complaints and assured us that they would do all they could to prepare for the wedding. I also called Miriam's parents, Uncle Sola and Aunty Lara, and the joy that beamed from them was so wonderful. They had always prayed for me, and it did not matter that they had big plans for their daughter's wedding. They immediately said they'd make mine a priority as well. This melted my heart, and my conversation with them was my final confirmation that God was involved, and our wedding dates had been signed and sealed in heaven as well as on Earth. Our friends and family were in support, so we officially started planning our wedding.

With all that settled, we began planning our lives with more precision. Yes, planning our wedding was important, especially to me, but we put even more effort into working towards a Christ-centered marriage and future together.

We immediately began marriage counseling at my church, and this is something I highly recommend to any newly engaged couple. We thoroughly enjoyed our counselling sessions and covered many important topics, including finances, managing in-laws, communication, sex, and many others. The sessions triggered even deeper conversations between us outside the class. It was helpful to understand some of the differences in males and females.

We enrolled in another counselling course at a different church to eradicate any biases; listened to Christian podcasts; watched videos; and read books on marriage, understanding our uniqueness, communication, and resolving conflicts. All this helped set our foundation, as it was paramount to us that Christ be infused in our home and our hearts always. One of Sanmi's many favorite quotes is, "If we are not learning, we are not growing; and if we are not growing, we are dying." Therefore, a commitment to learning and growing is one of the standards we live by.

Our First Home

Owning a home was always one of my goals, mainly as an investment, and I had started working towards this even before Sanmi came along. Now that we were kicking off plans for our wedding, we agreed to buy our first home before our ceremonies took place. We wanted to ensure that we would make wise use of our resources, rather than splurging and spending everything on the wedding or other, less important, things. After exploring various home options, we quickly agreed that building a brand-new home would be a more futuristic goal, which we could pursue when we were more settled and as our little family began to grow. I leaned more towards townhomes for convenience, and Sanmi was interested in a single-family home. Since I still lived in Rochester, I wasn't physically present at most of the home showings he attended, but I joined in virtually.

While I was away, Sanmi, Mimi, and ID had come across a property just a block away from where Mimi and ID lived. They felt it was a great option, as it was within our budget. This wasn't necessarily the neighborhood we had in mind, but it was a central area, so the crew decided to make inquiries. Unfortunately, the seller had pulled the property off the market.

We decided to explore other options, and it was beginning to get exhausting. We weren't having any luck finding the perfect home while also staying within budget. A few weeks later, we decided to put an offer in for a townhouse that we kind of liked. I had come down to Minneapolis to do a walk-through of the townhouse with Sanmi, and we agreed we would settle for it since we hadn't found a single-family home that would work.

As I drove back to Rochester that night, Mimi called to tell me the house in her neighborhood was just put back on the market that day. I was so confused, because we had just put in an offer on the townhome we'd visited. I immediately called Sanmi, and he felt it was not a coincidence. He reached out to our realtor and scheduled a showing to view the property the next day.

Sanmi called me virtually during the showing, beaming with joy. He was convinced that this was our home. The realtor pulled out of our previous offer and put in another for this property. As God would have it, our offer was accepted the same day, the home was appraised for a few thousand lower than our offer, and the necessary funds were available. Everything worked together for our good, and exactly six months to our big day, we closed on our first home.

You may be thinking, "Wow, buying a home together before getting married?" Well, that is fair, and looking from the outside, I would probably think that, too. This is yet another reason why it is critical to be in tune with the Holy Spirit and ensure that you are guided and instructed by him—not by what you feel is right or what seems appropriate. Sanmi and I prayed throughout our decision process, and we had every sense of peace to go ahead with this move. Although we hadn't had our wedding ceremonies yet, we believed we were ordained to be man and wife by God and had all the direction and confidence in God to purchase our first home. So, we did. Buying our home was the first item I checked off on our wedding planning list.

What Do We Do?

There was just one question. Since we'd bought a home in Minneapolis, but I lived and worked ninety miles away in Rochester, how was this going to work? Would I have to drive almost two hours each way every day? Would I live in this house all by myself until the wedding? Would I stay in Rochester where I paid rent, but also have a mortgage in Minneapolis? What the heck were we going to do?

Although we had all these unknowns and so many questions lingering, we somehow remained calm and continued to be full of gratitude for an undeserved blessing, especially when we had a huge expense ahead of us.

Trust in the Lord with all your heart and lean not on your own understanding; in all your ways submit to him, and he will make your paths straight.

— PROVERBS 3:5-6 (NIV)

This scripture carried us through every decision we had made so far. The truth is, some of it didn't make sense, but we went ahead, trusting God to take care of us every step of the way.

Just a handful of people knew we had bought our home. To diffuse any reasons for concern, we thought it was best to make sure we had figured out a plan and at least were able to answer some of our own questions before we shared with family and friends. We were still in the process of figuring things out when Sanmi shared rather shocking news. It was a bombshell that brought about a mixture of emotions.

Sanmi had been job-searching, as he really wanted a full-time position in his field. While he was getting his master's in Business Administration at the University of Massachusetts, one of his instructors had encouraged him to apply for a program called Changing the Face of Tech. This program provided opportunities for bright minds to get acquainted with STEM (Science, Technology, Engineering, and Math) jobs. As part of this program, Sanmi had an opportunity to go with peers to explore a reputable tech organization that had a facility in Franklin, Massachusetts and meet with the leaders of the organization. Sanmi had made a remarkable impression on the leaders he met, and they'd contacted him to see if he was interested in interviewing for a position. Unknown to me, he had applied for the position and gone through the interview process.

On this particular evening, he broke the news that he had gotten a fantastic job. He shared what his salary would be, and I screamed, jumped, danced, and thanked God for this great testimony. I was in awe of God, as Sanmi was starting off well. Then, Sanmi told me the job would require him to relocate back to Boston. For about a minute, I was numb. I lost every sensation in my body.

I had so many questions but was unsure where to begin. I was super happy and thankful to God for answering our prayers of Sanmi getting a full-time job in his field, but he had to move?

We'd just bought this house. What were we going to do? We were planning our wedding, still courting and getting to know each other, still learning, growing, and preparing for marriage How was all this supposed to play out with Sanmi moving back to Boston? I was not sure how to express all these emotions at once.

Sanmi was certain that I had nothing to worry about. He didn't know how things were going to play out, but he encouraged me to be still and trust God. Somehow, it would all work out for our good. I braced myself and celebrated with him.

The weeks began to fly by. Shortly before it was time for him to go, I held a little surprise going-away dinner to celebrate his accomplishment. Sanmi is an excellent guy and truly deserved this great opportunity. He had been so calm and optimistic throughout his job search. Not once did he complain or express fear or doubt. His positivity was so contagious, and it helped me remain positive through it all. We planned to stay in constant communication. He would fly down as often as he could, I would fly over as often as I could, we would meet up in other states whenever possible, and we would make the best of our hopefully short long-distance courtship.

He Always Comes Through

Sanmi was gone. I was shuttling between Rochester and Minneapolis, adjusting to my long-distance courtship, and in full wedding planning mode. One day at work, I was walking down the hallway and spotted my department director in his office. The Holy Spirit immediately prompted me to go have a word with him about my commute to work. I was hesitant because he was my boss's boss, and I felt it would be more appropriate to speak with my direct boss first. I felt unsettled in my spirit as I walked past his office, so I decided to go back.

I knocked, and he asked me to come in and have a seat. I caught him up a little on how things were going at work, then explained that I had recently moved from Rochester and had been commuting.

"It really has been stressful," I said, "and I'd like to explore options for working at the Mayo Clinic Sports Medicine office in downtown Minneapolis."

He was very empathetic and said he could imagine how difficult that must be for me. He clarified that the Sports Medicine office might not be an option, as it was a more clinical space. However, he pointed out that a great option might be an office space Mayo leased in Eagan, which is only about thirty minutes from Minneapolis. He advised me to contact another project manager who previously worked in that office to ensure that it was still available. If it was, he said I could certainly work from there. If not, we could explore other options.

I did as I was told, and in a week, my bag-packing and commuting were over. I was allowed to work from the Eagan office as long as I committed to going to Rochester once a week in order to stay engaged with my team. Soon, I was officially back living in Minneapolis.

Before moving, Sanmi had done a lot of work with our contractors, renovating our home. Together, we took our renovation project one day at a time as I began to settle in our new home. The news of my job relocation made him so happy. We both felt it was a confirmation that God was indeed ordering our steps.

Sanmi was not very comfortable with my living alone in the house. Since my brother was in the process of moving out of his place, we suggested that he stay with me until we figured out where we would settle, or at least until after our wedding, which was six months away. Lasun was fine with this idea, and Sanmi was now at peace. Day by day, week by week, month by month, all of our puzzle pieces continued to align perfectly.

The Cherry on the Sundae

A few months had passed since my hubby-to-be and I had begun a long-distance courtship. Contrary to popular belief and some of my initial fears, the distance didn't cause us to drift apart in any way. In fact, it brought us a lot closer. Since we were not together physically, we became very intentional about the quality of time we spent together, either when we spoke on the phone, talked virtually, or visited. We communicated a lot and had resolvable arguments.

Sanmi had never been involved in any wedding or event planning, so we had quite a lot to discuss and argue about regarding the wedding plans. Many things came as a shock to him, especially the cost of wedding-related items. In one of our late-night conversations, he said he knew how important our wedding and marriage were to me and understood that it was an occasion I had planned for and dreamed of for a long time. He made a commitment to support me and give his all to ensure that I would be happy on my wedding day and beyond. It was one of the most heartfelt and sacrificial things Sanmi had done— yet another indication of how deeply he loved me and that he was willing to love me with all that he had.

We had a lot of fun planning our wedding. When we were together, I would make Sanmi watch wedding videos on YouTube, just so he'd have an idea how these types of events go. Those sessions were like torture for him, and his commentary, facial expressions, and reactions were always priceless. After buying and renovating our house, planning our wedding was our second big project together, and this further solidified our relationship and helped us develop a team mindset. We were both always working towards the same goal, and we quickly identified that we functioned best together. I began to have a better understanding of the scripture, "Two people are better off than one, for they can help each other succeed. If one person falls, the other can reach out and help.

But someone who falls alone is in real trouble" (Ecclesiastes 4:9-10 NLT).

We were reading together, learning and growing together, spending quality time together, being intentional about the quality of our conversations, and resolving any disagreements within the same conversation or on the same day By God's grace, we have still never held a grudge or carried any misunderstanding over to the next day. As we kept at this, we were praying and trusting God for direction on where we would settle after our wedding. We agreed that, whatever the case, we did not want to live apart after our wedding. Though we didn't have any clear direction on how it would all work out, we were heavily dependent on God and trusted that he would sort us out.

When Sanmi was offered his job in Boston, he had told his boss that he would be getting married and his family was in Minnesota. He was told that he needed to work in Boston during his probation period, since he needed to become familiarized with his team and leaders and get acclimated to the organization's culture. After about three months, his performance would be evaluated, and he might be able to relocate and work from the facility in Minnesota. This gave us hope.

Before we knew it, Sanmi had been away a little over three months, our wedding was about two months away, and we had it —the cherry on our sundae, the icing on our cake, or whatever extra-sweet topping you can get on something that is already sweet. Sanmi had met his boss for his evaluation, he had surpassed expectations, he was loved and admired at work and he was granted his request to work from the Minnesota office. They said he could start there by the end of the year. Just like that, God once again settled us. In a situation where we had absolutely no idea how things would turn out, all of our faith, hope, and trust were solely rooted in Christ, and he who sees the end from the beginning had it all figured out. All we needed to do was trust him.

After our wedding ceremonies, we planned to have a week-long honeymoon in Mexico during the first week of December. Sanmi would go back to Boston to wrap things up at work and officially finalize his relocation, then he would move back home permanently right before Christmas, and we would begin to live happily ever after. This, for us, remains a huge testimony. Just like Psalms 16:6 says, "The lines have fallen to me in pleasant places; Yes, I have a good inheritance" (NKJV). Lines had indeed fallen unto us in pleasant places.

I pray that this encourages you to trust God in every situation, even when you don't know how things will work out. This is certainly one of the hardest things to do. That, I can definitely attest to. It is also why, as brothers and sisters in Christ, we should encourage and uplift one another to keep faith and trust God. He works all things out in our favor if we are obedient and set our gazes on him.

If we make decisions by our own intuition, the outcome may lead to destruction, as highlighted in Proverbs 14:12. "There is a way which seems right to a man and appears straight before him, But its end is the way of death" (AMP). Rather, let's strive to have an open, honest dialogue with God, saying, "Lord, here are my thoughts and plans. Do they align with yours? What will you have me do? Not my will, but yours be done, o Lord!" Seeking God and being patient enough to hear his response solidifies our relationship with him, and it confirms our total dependence on him.

> Trust in the Lord with all your heart;
>> do not depend on your own understanding.
>> Seek his will in all you do,
>> and he will show you which path to take.
>
> — PROVERBS 3:5-6 (NLT)

The LORD directs the steps of the godly. He delights in every detail of their lives.

— PSALMS 37:23 (NLT)

But the path of the just (righteous) is like the light of dawn, that shines brighter and brighter until [it reaches its full strength and glory in] the perfect day.

— (PROVERBS 4:18 AMP)

Reflection and Prayer

Write down some areas of your life in which you are unsure what to do or need direction on how to proceed. Today, decide to lean on God's understanding and trust him to guide you through the situation:

Father, I submit to you: ___ (Insert your upcoming decision).

CHAPTER 12

GRATITUDE FOR MY DREAM WEDDING

I have decided to share this portion of my story because I was able to draw many lessons from it, and I believe you might find value in it as well. It sums up the manifestation of God's power, concludes one phase of my life's journey, and ushers me into a new chapter with a new story to be told.

I am reminded, time and time again, that there is nothing too big, too small, too mundane, too weird, too vain, too *anything* to pray to God about. It is important to understand that every good desire of our hearts is valid, and if something is important to us, then it is important to God.

One of my favorite analogies compares us with a little child. The things that amuse children may not amuse us. A child will often laugh so hard at the sounds a new toy makes. Once we notice that this toy makes our kid happy, we buy her the upgraded version or the next possible gadget that could make her even happier. This toy isn't amusing to us, but since our child finds it desirable, we provide it in abundance. We may also make note of a toy the child points to in the store. She'll cry and sometimes throw a tantrum if her parent refuses to buy the toy she wants, not realizing that the parent has good reasons. Either the child is not old enough for that toy yet, or the parent has plans already to surprise her with it on her birthday.

This is exactly how our almighty God responds to our good desires. We are his babies, and he is our parent. He makes our happiness and needs a priority. As long as we ask, he wants to give us what we have asked for. He could choose to grant our request right when we ask for it, decide to give it to us at a more appropriate time, or surprise us with it at a time unknown to us, especially when he knows that delay will be better for us.

God probably had a huge smile on his face during all the years I spent planning my wedding by faith—dreaming of my wedding ceremony and saving pictures, ideas, and colors. He may not even have understood why I was so detailed about this event in my life. He must have made a decision to bring that dream to fruition at his own appointed time, when he alone would take all the glory. Psalms 37:4 says, "Delight yourself in the LORD, And he will give you the desires of your heart" (ESV).

Since I am passionate about the institution of marriage, I absolutely love weddings and desired to have one—some people don't, and it is absolutely fine. I planned my wedding by faith even before I came close to meeting my fiancé. On many occasions, I saw myself as a bride and practiced my dance. I celebrated with others and shared in their joy, with all the confidence in my heart that one day my dream would become a reality. I didn't know when God would do it or how he would do it, but with God, *impossible* is nothing. Scripture reminds us that, "[...] with man this is impossible, but with God all things are possible" (Matthew 19:26 NIV).

The Wedding Planning Project

Since our wedding would be taking place in Nigeria, and I didn't live there, I depended heavily on Instagram and referrals from friends in deciding on vendors. I knew that having a wedding planner would be essential, but I had no clue how to go about securing one. I prayed about it, and not too long afterward, I randomly remembered the wedding scene in the season finale of one of my favorite Nigerian comedy web series *Skinny Girl in Transit*. That wedding was beautiful, intimate, and nicely decorated, exactly the type of church wedding I wanted. I did some Instagram research and found that Etal Events had planned the wedding scene. I said to myself, "I have found my wedding planner."

I located the CEO's phone number and gave her a call, starting the conversation with, "Hello, you're my wedding planner."

I bet she was confused, probably thinking, *I am?*

We chatted for about an hour as though we had been friends since high school. I felt at total peace speaking with her and sharing my thoughts and ideas. She understood me even before I went into the nitty gritty details. For every idea or thought I had, Sike sent me pictures of similar work she had done to confirm that we were on the same page, and she understood my thought process.

I felt confident that she was suitable for the job and just what I needed when planning outside of the country. At the time, she was in America, which allowed us to speak more frequently. It was that easy. I didn't shop around or go through a long list of options before deciding. I sought God's help, and he directed me right where I needed to be, hassle-free.

My Dress

Another interesting adventure was picking out my wedding dress. I've always wanted something modest but still subtly sexy. I also wanted something simple and classy, nothing extra or over-the-top, since I would probably never wear the dress again after the wedding.

I went wedding dress shopping on two occasions. First was with Priyanka. I tried on a few pretty dresses but nothing that really felt like the right one. It was a fun experience, since it was my first time trying on wedding dresses. A few months later, I visited the stores again, with Mimi and Tosin connected virtually. I tried on the most beautiful dresses and, in some of them, felt like a bride, like a true princess. I danced in front of the mirrors, wore a veil, held a bouquet, and did the whole shebang! It really began to hit me again that, this time, I was the bride, not a bridesmaid. I finally tried on a dress that was everything I wanted, but with much more bling than I needed. It was absolutely stunning and flattering on my body but a lot more elaborate and expensive than I had planned. So, unfortunately, I couldn't say yes to the dress.

Later that night, I thought about the dress a lot, but I couldn't justify spending that much on a wedding dress even if I could afford it. I decided to look up the brand of the dress online and came across what I called the *little sister* of that gorgeous dress. It had the same lace and crystals, but the bustle wasn't as elaborate. It also wasn't bedazzled. It was simple, yet so elegant. The best part was the price, a fourth of the initial dress's cost, and there it was on the internet! I'd found my dress. I just needed to figure out how to see it in person, to make sure it was as beautiful as I had imagined.

I called all the bridal stores I could find in Minnesota, and not a single store had it available. Finally, I came across one that was willing to order a sample from the manufacturer for a small fee. If I still loved it after seeing it in person, then they could order it in my color and size. After a few weeks, I got a call that the sample had arrived. I couldn't wait to see the dress in person.

I was not at all disappointed. It was even more beautiful in person than I had imagined. It was simple but elegant, conservative—which was what I wanted—but the mesh sleeves and back gave it some sexiness. It was right on budget, and I would get it two months before the wedding. So, right then, I placed an order.

I shopped around for a cathedral veil, and the ones I came

across were either flimsy or way too pricey. I tasked Sayo with helping me find a veil, since she is resourceful and fashionable. She got the most beautiful veil, subtle yet so classy, just what I had envisioned myself wearing, and it matched my wedding dress perfectly. Sayo refused payment for the veil and gifted it to me for my wedding, a totally unexpected gesture.

My Mom

There has never been a single doubt in my heart how deeply my mom loves my brother and me. She has sacrificed and prayed for us so much, and still does. However, I experienced a whole new type of love from her as I prepared for my wedding. Besides God, my mom was my number one supporter and confidant from the second I started planning my wedding. She worked closely with my planner to pick out the best wedding venues, caterers, and so on. She coordinated with my in-laws to pick the clothes for the wedding and went to all my consultations, cake tastings, dress fittings, everything! She tried to make sure I was happy with all the decisions made. If I made any requests or changes, she would end by saying, "As long as you're happy." I had never experienced such selflessness and love. Planning my wedding made me value my mom more than I ever had.

Many times, I imagined how things would have turned out if I didn't have my mom's love and support. Honestly, I wouldn't have been able to pull it off. One huge eye-opener for me was that no family member or friend could love me or sacrifice for me the way my mother would. I'd learned the hard way to never expect anything from anybody, because that leads to hurtful disappointment. Our only ever-present friend is God, the sure one who never forsakes or disappoints. God fully had my back, and my mommy didn't forsake or disappoint me, either, even when I was naughty.

Mom and I certainly did bump heads in some areas, because moms will always be moms. Mama knows best, right? Well, in some areas, I was certain *I* knew best, and no one could tell me otherwise. My mom worried so much about offending people if we didn't invite them to the wedding. I, on the other hand, was okay with certain people being offended, because I knew they would be invited to another wedding the following weekend and would completely forget about mine. Since I wanted my mom to be honored and celebrated at my wedding, I was okay with her inviting everyone she wanted to my traditional ceremony, but having a small intimate church wedding was the agreement I had made with God. I was determined to stick to that. Each time Mom submitted her guestlist, we went through a negotiation process until we were able to meet in the middle. She continued to confirm to me that, regardless of her ideas and opinions, she wanted me to be happy.

With my consent, my mom booked a band for the traditional ceremony. About a month before the wedding, I came across another band that I instantly fell in love with. I wanted a fully Christian band, because I wanted God to be glorified even through the festivities and celebrations. I felt strongly that this band would do an excellent job, so I reached out to the artist who led the band, Laolu Gbenjo, and he was going to charge more, even after I had negotiated my lungs out. I asked God to help me break this news to my mom. I went to her with a presentation, and many videos of his performances, and did everything in my power to convince her that he would be a fantastic choice. She decided to do her own research, after which she confirmed it was a great choice. She was willing to forfeit the deposit she had paid to the previous band just to make me happy. I was truly touched by the sacrifice.

The humility my mom exudes is one for the books. She is so Godly, so down-to-Earth, so selfless, so generous, so loving, and so *forgiving*. I emphasize forgiveness because I have seen how she lives out the principle of forgiving seventy times, according to Matthew 18:21-22. "Then Peter came up and said to him, 'Lord, how often shall my brother sin against me, and I forgive him? As many as seven times?' Jesus said to him, 'I do not say to you seven times, but seventy times seven'" (RSV).

For every time I was rude, disrespectful, opinionated, moody, indecisive, or whatever the case was, my mom never held it against me. She never told me to go figure it out myself, held a grudge, or talked down on me. She always forgave. She overlooked so many things, forgave people time and time again, and gave generously to so many.

She did not take over my wedding, despite how much she put into it. She ensured that my husband and I would enjoy our day. At one point during the festivities, I wondered where she was and why she wasn't partying with us on the dance floor. She was busy making sure everything and everyone else was okay. She didn't make it about herself but about us. She gave her all, expecting nothing in return.

I was not just lucky, but truly blessed to be birthed by my mom, and that is a blessing I will never take for granted. I pray daily that she will live in excellent health, peace, and wealth to enjoy the fruits of the seeds she has sewn in my life and the lives of so many around her. I pray that God will adorn her with his crown of glory.

My Grandma

I cannot give all the applause to my mom without giving credit to God and to the woman who birthed her and raised us both, Christiana Jokotade Coker. Having my grandma alive and in perfect health to witness my wedding was another of my biggest testimonies. Every time I prayed that God would bless me with a husband, I followed it with a prayer that my grandma would witness it. The Lord—who does exceedingly, abundantly, above all that we could ask or think—didn't just keep my grandma alive. She was, and still is, in perfect health. She was the most beautiful grandmother-of-the-bride I had ever seen.

Shortly after her eightieth birthday in 2018, she fell ill, and we feared losing her. But God—Jehovah Rapha, the greatest healer—and Dr. Jesus, as my grandma would call him, came to her rescue and restored her health.

She has prayed for me throughout my entire life. Even when I was a little girl, she prayed that God would choose a spouse for me and place me in a wonderful family. She raised me in the church and taught me the importance of Godliness, cleanliness, and being industrious. When I was a child, she ensured that I stood in the kitchen while she cooked, made me do chores, and taught me the importance of education. I wanted all her desires and prayers over me to manifest in her lifetime, and by God's grace, it was happening.

My grandma called almost every day leading up to my wedding to pray with me. When I went to Nigeria briefly to make some of the preparations, she would call me into her room to share wisdom with me, advising me to love and respect my husband and to also love and respect my in-laws. She advised me to be mindful of friends, because not all who called themselves friends would truly wish me well or be happy for me. She emphasized that I must share all of my worries and problems with God, and God alone, not even her or my mom. We had many counselling sessions, and she represented my dear grandfather, Chief Emmanuel Oladehinde Coker, who I know would have been so proud to see me get married. My grandma gave generously towards my wedding and rallied her family members and church members to celebrate with her. I saw nothing but pure joy, fulfilment, and pride in my grandmother's eyes on my wedding day.

I always pray that, just as my desire came true for her to witness my wedding, God continues to keep her in perfect health so she will see all my children and witness the weddings of all her other grandchildren.

My Brother

My big brother and only sibling, Lasun Olagboye, was my backbone and sounding board throughout my wedding process. He patiently listened to my rants and checked in almost daily to see how things were going. He was not just in touch with me, but also stayed connected with our mom and my husband-to-be throughout the planning process. Although he didn't know much about weddings, he was willing to listen, look things up, and give his opinions on different aspects.

He also acted as liaison between my mom and me when we didn't see eye to eye. He would constantly tell me, "You know she is old. You have to be patient with her," or "You know she cares about culture. Just don't argue with her. Say you've heard and do what you want. She will eventually adjust." My brother has a really calm personality—we're opposites in that regard—so he does a better job calming me down when Mom and I are cross with each other.

My brother supported us tremendously as we planned our wedding, although he wasn't able to attend the ceremonies in person. He made enormous financial contributions, was fully involved, and has remained an integral part of our lives. My prayer for him is that God will constantly remain his pillar of support and backbone. God has appointed him head of the Olagboye family and will meet him daily at every point of need.

My Uncles, Aunties, and Cousins

My maternal uncles, aunties, and cousins, and the Cokers and the Adisa gang—when I think of family, they are the ones I mean. My mom has three brothers, and their sibling relationship is out of this world. They are very close-knit, love and support one another, and would go to the ends of the Earth for each other. They share the same bond with their first cousins, the Adisa brothers in London, and I am a huge beneficiary of the love they all share. My uncles, their spouses, and all their children flew all the way from Minnesota and London for my wedding, a financial sacrifice I am not able to fathom. It did not matter who else was present, as long as I had the "Adiscos," I had all the support I needed. Their show of love was immeasurable, and having them all present boosted my mom's morale and confidence. She didn't feel alone.

These were the other people who raised me, because I had spent many years of my life living with my uncles in Minnesota. People would tease me as the "girl with many homes," because all of their doors were open to me. While I studied in the UK, my uncles in London and their spouses were my guardians. I participated in their family vacations, and they constantly prayed for me.

Just six months before, this entire clan had flown to London and Malta to attend Miriam and John's wedding, but here they all were again at mine! I fully understand, now, that family is everything.

I always pray that nothing and no one will ever disrupt the love and bond my family shares, and that God will be a constant support to every member of the Coker and Adisa families.

My In-Laws

I didn't fully understand the importance of praying for and about in-laws until the Lord placed me in the Awujoola family. In the chapter where we discussed the types of prayers I prayed before marriage, I mentioned the ways I prayed for my in-laws. I have never seen a more Godly, loving, humble, or subtle set of individuals. The love and support we received from the Awujoola and Olowoyo families were astounding.

Sanmi's mom passed away when he was only two years old. He is the last of six children, with four older brothers and a sister who is the eldest. Sister Kemi, who we fondly call "The Sis," gave her all to ensure that our wedding was successful. Our sis and her husband checked in on us throughout the planning. Although they were also here in Minnesota, which restricted how much they could do for a wedding in Nigeria, they participated in the planning process.

I honor, salute, and celebrate my newly adopted dad, Professor Afolabi Awujoola. He didn't just bless me with a fantastic husband, but he raised exceptional children. I have total respect for him. Daddy counselled us on several occasions, teaching and feeding us with God's word. He also continually reminded us that our wedding was a day's event, but our marriage is a lifetime. We should, therefore, ensure that we invest much more in our lives *after* the wedding instead of just in the wedding. Daddy also gave generously towards our wedding, and the pride and joy on his face on our wedding day was so contagious.

My union with Sanmi is a complete blessing for both of us. God didn't just bless me with a husband, but with a dad, too. He also blessed Sanmi with a mom, restoring to each of us a parent we had lost.

The love Sanmi and his siblings share is adorable, and they have extended all that love to me. Sanmi's brothers ran around Nigeria tirelessly to provide everything we needed for our traditional wedding. Even though planning a wedding did not come naturally to them, which is typical of most men, they went over and beyond, touching base several times with Sanmi and me to make sure whatever they bought was exactly what we wanted. They continued to assure me that all was fine, and I had absolutely nothing to worry about. Sister Kemi would often tell me to choose whatever I wanted for the wedding and just send her the bill. As long as it made me happy, she was satisfied with it. Despite her busy schedule, she would check in with my mom in Nigeria to get up to speed on how things were going. She and her husband contributed financially to our wedding, in addition to blessing us with many gifts.

Sanmi's immediate older brother had just gotten married

three months before our wedding, but the entire family supported and blessed us with gifts, money, and prayers. Although Sanmi's mom was not present, Sister Kemi did an absolutely phenomenal job ensuring that she was well represented. Her sisters were present, and her mom, Sanmi's grandmother, was able to witness our wedding at age 103.

I am eternally grateful to God for placing me in such a wonderful family. My prayer is that the bond of love the family shares will never be broken, and Christ will forever remain the pillar and firm foundation of our family.

My Pastors

I was only fifteen years old when I first joined the City of Strong Tower Parish, now called Christ Family Kingdom Center for All Nations. It was in this church that I rededicated my life and began a consistent walk with God under the leadership of Pastor Emmanuel Olowokere, popularly known as Pastor Sola. He sowed seeds that grew me spiritually, not only through his Sunday teachings, but by the manner in which he conducted himself.

Pastor Sola isn't just a pastor to me. He is a father, grandpa to our future children, mentor, and friend. He is one of the most humble, generous, and kindhearted individuals I have ever met. He finds a way to connect with everyone on a personal level, taking a true interest and living out his vision of building not just spiritual individuals, but spiritual Kingdom families. Pastor Sola and his wife, Pastor Jumoke, have been model spiritual parents, who lead by example and instill Godly values in everyone they come across. One of my fondest memories of Pastor Sola was a boat ride he and I went on during a church retreat. While we were in the boat, I asked if he would be my dad. He accepted my proposal and has played the role excellently.

Just seven days before I met Sanmi, Pastor Sola called me on two different occasions during the Praise festival at church and said confidently, "You will be getting married very soon." Both times he said it, I agreed with him and laughed at God's sense of humor, because the only prayer request I had made for myself throughout that Praise festival was that God would bless me with my husband. With great joy, I eventually shared the news of my relationship with my Pastor. He asked to meet with Sanmi and adopted him as a son. He was confident that this was, indeed, the Lord's doing, and his approval was another confirmation for me that Sanmi was my God-ordained husband.

Pastor Sola was one of the strongest support systems we had from the beginning of our courtship. Throughout our wedding planning process, he was always just a phone call away, backing us up like any true and loving father would. He ended every conversation by praying for us. Likewise, Pastor Jumoke often checked in to see how things were coming along.

Pastor Sola had open, honest conversations with us, asked questions, and took genuine interest in our plans. He never let me complete a sentence of complaint. He would always interrupt by saying, "Daughter, I told you not to worry about anything. Did I not tell you not to worry?"

Pastor Sola and Pastor Jumoke are the most giving, loving and sacrificial spiritual parents. Although Pastor Sola always assured me that one or both of them would be in attendance at our wedding, I was a bit skeptical, because our church wedding occurred on the US Thanksgiving Holiday. Understanding how important this holiday is to most families, I feared that it would take precedence over the wedding ceremony. Pastor Sola and Pastor Jumoke kept to their word, and Pastor Sola represented the Olowokere family at the wedding. They made a huge sacrifice for us, contributed generously to our wedding, and covered us always in prayers.

Pastor Sola went over and beyond to ensure that we had an excellent church wedding ceremony. He made sure Sanmi and I arrived at the church venue in style. The message he preached on our wedding day, titled "Who Is on Your Guestlist?" is one I will never forget. He admonished us to do nothing in life without having Christ as the guest of honor. Having him join Sanmi and me in holy matrimony was an honor, a dream come true, and an answered prayer. It gave me so much joy to see the happiness and pride on his face that day. He said on several occasions, "I am very proud of you." Those were not words I'd heard often in my life, especially from any father figure. This is one of the many reasons I consider him not just a Pastor, but a father whom I regard highly.

Words continue to fail me in expressing the depth of my gratitude. No gifts can measure up, but my prayer remains that God's unending grace and mercy will continue to be their portion. I pray that God will reward Pastor Sola and Pastor Jumoke bountifully, and that, as they've taken joy and pride in us as spiritual children, they will have immeasurable joy and pride in all their biological children.

My Friends

About eight weeks before my wedding, a few of my friends held the most beautiful, classy, and tasteful bridal shower I had ever attended. I was completely blown away, as they had taken bridal showers to a totally different level. They had withheld all of the planning information from me, and to be honest, I wanted no part in planning my bridal shower. I didn't want anything in particular and had my mind and hands full with planning the wedding. I was sometimes skeptical about having a bridal shower, because I didn't want anyone to be burdened, especially my bridesmaids, since my wedding was taking place out of the country. Tosin and Mimi kept me excited about the shower and continually told me it wasn't for me to worry about.

Tosin encouraged me to get something nice to wear and made many efforts to keep me in high spirits for the occasion. It turned out more beautiful than I'd imagined, and the love and support I received were mind-blowing. I found out that Simi, who lives in Canada, had taken my bridal shower so personally, although she couldn't be there. She stayed engaged, not just with me to make sure things were going well with the wedding plans, but also with my friends. She had a vision of the ambiance she wanted for my shower, and she didn't care what it would cost. She hired a great decorator and covered the cost of a beautifully decorated venue. All my friends contributed to making sure I had a beautiful and memorable bridal shower.

I had five bridesmaids, all but one of whom lived in America. So, Mimi, Tosin, Tope, and Sayo had to fly all the way to Nigeria. In fact, I didn't think Tope would make it for my wedding, since she'd just gone to Nigeria a month before for her dad's birthday. She insisted that she wouldn't miss my wedding for anything.

Jumoke, who was the only bridesmaid living in Nigeria, was my eyes and ears out there. She called me almost every day, following up on statuses, went wedding venue hunting on my behalf, and even had meetings with my mom to make sure we secured the best venues. Jumoke and her mom handcrafted and designed all my wedding invitations and charged almost nothing. I could trust Jumoke with my funds, so she kept all the money for all my wedding vendors till all deposits and balances were completely paid, meticulously keeping a proper account of every expenditure.

Sayo checked in from time to time to make sure things were going well with the planning, and as I mentioned earlier, got me the most beautiful wedding veil.

Mimi, of course, wore so many hats—sister of the bride, Maid of Honor, bridesmaid coordinator, bride's coordinator, you name it. All of these hats, she wore effortlessly and with no complaints. She had looked forward to my wedding as much as I had.

Finally, Tosin was that friend and bridesmaid whom God strategically placed in my life in the most essential season. She was a solid backbone and voice of reason as I prepared for my wedding. Tosin, who is a wife, mother of two, and a full-time career woman, always somehow made time to be there for me. She made it a priority to ensure that I was excited as I planned my wedding. Sometimes, I didn't understand why she was my "Ginger girl" and biggest cheerleader. She just always wanted me to enjoy the process. Tosin took initiative every step of the way. Even when I would say I didn't need help with anything, she would come around anyway to be present with me. When we finally arrived in Nigeria for the wedding, she would call to ask where I was, and she would just show up to be there with me. She was and has remained a real blessing to me.

I had the best bridesmaids, who didn't just look absolutely stunning, but surrounded and showered me with love on my wedding day. They bent over backwards for me without any complaints. On the day of the occasion, I felt well supported.

All of my older friends, who are like big sisters to me, rallied round me and gave their support in every way possible. When I introduced Sanmi to each of them, the feedback was almost universal. They were first relieved that I was about to be married, then they were overjoyed and soon transferred their affection for me to him.

Titi took on the sourcing of my traditional clothes and sharing ideas on social media. On countless occasions, she would say, "Yimika, you have to look nice. Another sister, Misi, was also involved every step of the way. She helped curate most of the wedding stationary and even gave monetary gifts. Sadly, her mom passed away in the same period, but it didn't dim her spirit in cheerfully supporting me. She flew all the way to Nigeria to be present on my big day, a gesture I deeply appreciate. These big sisters, just to name a few, stayed involved in the planning of the wedding and contributed a lot toward our expenses as well. My marriage was a dream come true for them all. Their joy was contagious. My prayer is that God blesses each and every one abundantly with all that they ask of him and much more.

All of my close friends from outside the country who, for valid reasons, couldn't physically be at my wedding ensured that

I didn't feel their absence a single bit. They showered me with so much love, prayer, gifts, and emotional support. Dolapo called me early in the morning to watch me get ready on my wedding day virtually. Ekan constantly reminded me to not get stressed and enjoy my day to the fullest. The love and support I received from all over the world was overwhelming.

Reflection and Prayer

Think of the people in your life who have supported or encouraged you through the great times of celebration or through challenging times. Thank God for them.

CHAPTER 13

MY WEDDING DAYS

It was finally time for me to make an entrance into my traditional wedding ceremony. I had been sitting in the car for about an hour, waiting to be called in. The band was playing, the saxophonist was blowing, and I stepped out of the car and walked to the engagement hall. A chill ran along my entire spine, and I busted out in tears. Most of my adulthood friends, all of my high school friends, all my cousins, and many members of my church—all the way from America—were gathered at the entrance, waiting to dance in with me. In all my years, I had never felt so loved and honored.

In that moment, I realized how meaningful relationships were and how colorful life is when we are surrounded by people we love. I saw firsthand the importance of belonging to a church family. I was so proud to be part of this great Kingdom family. Uncles, aunties, mummies and grandmas, who were members of my church, had come from far and wide to cheer me on. The outpouring of love from my church was truly immeasurable. My heart was filled with so much joy and gratitude, I didn't know how to express it. If I tried to name all those whom I appreciate, I would run out of pages, but for the rest of my life, I will remember the happiness that flowed through my veins when I saw everyone who came to share in my joy and support me. I will eternally be grateful.

All My Prayers Answered

Sanmi and I had made a commitment to worry about absolutely nothing on our wedding day. We were determined to give God our best praise, dance like David danced, and have the best time of our lives. We knew this was our only chance, because we were only going to get married once. We had spent many months planning, and it was time to finally enjoy the outcome. Absolutely nothing was going to stop that.

I was truly in awe as I stepped into the exquisitely decorated hall. It looked way more beautiful than I had imagined or asked for. Every surface held a layer of greenery and a burst of beautiful colors—pinks, maroons, gold. Everything was lush and radiant. For a second, I almost couldn't believe it was my wedding. Mike Aremu, who is one of the frontrunners of world-class saxophonists and an awesome worshiper, graced us with his presence and ushered me and my cheerleaders into the venue with notes of high praise.

I was filled with so many emotions. Each time my eyes watered, I would think about my false eyelashes and try to keep the tears from falling. I could feel the presence of so many people, but it seemed like I couldn't see anyone. I just sang the praise songs that were being played, and I danced with every breath in my body.

After a few minutes, my eyes cleared. Fireworks were going off, and family and friends joined me on the dance floor, showering money in different denominations and currencies on me. I was in heaven. The coordinator of the event asked if I was satisfied with the dancing and was ready to proceed with the event. Satisfied? Oh, yes. This was the absolute least I could give God, but I gave it with the whole of my heart.

I was ushered to kneel before my mom, who prayed wholeheartedly for me. By this time, I couldn't hold the tears back. It was a moment I'd looked forward to my whole life. I took pictures with my family, then was ushered to the Awujoola family. I was asked to wave goodbye to my family, and this made me cry even more. It was a rather nostalgic feeling, because I had been part of the Olagboye and Coker family my whole life and, just like that, it was time to leave that name behind. I was happy to cleave to my new family, but sad to be leaving my old one. Daddy Awujoola and Sister Kemi, who represented Sanmi's mom, welcomed me officially to the family and prayed for me.

The moment I had been waiting for had now come. My tears had dried up by the time I looked up at the wonderfully decorated stage. My Sanmi, my king, was sitting up there, looking dashing in his traditional attire, with the widest smile I had ever seen on his face. All of his teeth were visible. The ceremony coordinator instructed me to dance up to him.

His first words to me were, "Babe, this is the happiest day of my life. This is so much fun!"

My heart melted. Sanmi was such a happy groom, he didn't need to be cajoled to dance or smile or do anything. He was on board for everything. This stood out to me because, often when I have been a bridesmaid, either the bride or the groom needed to be cajoled or almost forced to smile, dance, or liven up. I understand that some people are shy, but I was very happy my Sanmi needed no encouragement. He danced, and it was apparent his joy truly came from within. That was quite understandable, because he'd definitely found a good thing (wink, wink). We both had a fantastic time and were thankful that the whole event didn't pass us by. We were able to fully take it in, be present, and enjoy our special day.

Our church wedding was next, a few days later. I had imagined myself walking down the aisle to many songs, but as that day drew closer, none of those songs fully captured how I felt. This was no longer an imaginary wedding or some type of fiction in my mind. I had a real fiancé and was going to walk down the aisle to him. Miraculously, I stumbled on the song "The One He Kept for Me" by Maurette Brown Clark. I bawled my eyes out as I listened to the lyrics over and over. I could relate to every word and was certain that the man I was about to marry was truly "the one I've waited for, my love's design, the one he kept for me until it was time." Making the decision to walk down the aisle to this song was easy.

Our church wedding was just as beautiful as the traditional one—all I'd hoped and prayed for and more. One of the greatest blessings for me was the honor of having my mother walk me down the aisle and give me away in marriage, another thing I'd prayed for. I watched Sanmi cry happy tears as I approached him. It sunk in that I was walking in with my mom and he and I would be walking out together, forever. In the midst of all the emotions that realization brought to the surface, my heart was at complete peace.

One of Nigeria's best gospel ministers, Mario Ese, ushered us into a powerful praise and worship session. It was a taste of heaven as we sang and worshipped God. I had requested the song "You made a way" by Travis Green, because God had moved every mountain and caused every wall to fall. We were all standing there *only* because God had made a way. Minister Ese and his praise band performed this song powerfully, and no doubt, Jesus was glorified.

The entire ceremony was everything I'd prayed for. Nothing was lacking. Every time Sanmi had a moment, he whispered in my ear how beautiful I looked or how much he loved me. My whole heart was full of joy and gratitude to God, as I was having the time of my life with the man of my dreams—my best friend and the best gift God had blessed me with. From the beginning of our relationship, Sanmi always made a promise to me, that wherever we were at that moment was the least of what we'd ever be. As he gave his vote of thanks and closing remarks, he made the same promise before our family and friends. "Babe," he said, "I promise you that this is the least we will ever be."

Oh, and I have one last wedding testimony. Remember how, on my list of things I prayed for, I'd wanted not just a beautiful wedding but a free one? Well, I testify to the glory of God that we were so thoroughly blessed financially, we had an *almost* free wedding. We were overwhelmed with cash gifts from so many people, it was unbelievable. For months and even more than a year after our wedding, we continued to receive financial gifts and recovered almost all that we had spent for the wedding.

It also dawned on me that I got married exactly a month before I turned thirty, a reality that had totally eluded me throughout the planning process. You may be thinking, "You were just thirty? What about those in their late thirties, forties, or even fifties who are yet to be married?" That's a valid question. As I mentioned in the beginning, I knew very early that one of my life's purposes was to make a positive impact on how people approach the institution of marriage. The longer it took for me to marry, the longer it took to fully live out that purpose. I also mentioned that when I drew my life's plan, I thought I was supposed to be married by age twenty-three and have kids by age twenty-five. I was still very single at age twenty-five. So, by my standards, I was delayed in my desire. The same timeline may not apply to others.

If you desire something today, depending on how badly you want it, if you don't get it almost right away, it can feel like an eternity even if you got it just a week later. After I reached age twenty-three, every year that I had to wait and trust God for my husband felt like eternity, and waiting was very painful. That delay didn't make sense to me until God's promise was made manifest. I finally understood why I had to wait and, in retrospect, if I had to wait even longer for the miracle and blessing I have today, it would be totally worth it. God's timing is always crucial. Wait for it, and your desire will surely come to pass. I remain in awe of God's great abilities.

When I say all of my prayers were answered, I mean every single request I took to God came to pass in my life—every single thing, big or mundane. God answered them all and blessed me with many more things I didn't even think to ask for. We actually did it, guys! But we are not done. The goal wasn't just to marry, but to glorify Jesus with and through our marriage.

Reflection and Prayer

Just like I had a clear picture of what I wanted in a husband, how I wanted my wedding to be, and the kind of marriage I desired, take some time to reflect and write exactly how you envision your miracle. Be as detailed as possible.

CHAPTER 14

A FINAL CHARGE ON APPLYING FAITH

I am a living testament to the truth that what God cannot do, does not exist. I am at a point in my life when I cannot be convinced otherwise. I have tested and tried him, and he has worked perfectly for me. I am certain that he can do much more for you, regardless of your circumstances, how long your wait has lasted, or what the world has said about your situation. The password is *faith*. You can evoke answers and grab God's attention simply by trusting in him, holding onto his word and promises, and having confidence within your heart that he is able to do all things and make life better than you imagined.

Some trust in chariots, and some in horses: but we will remember the name of the LORD our God.

— PSALMS 20:7 (KJV)

The scripture above is a pretty popular one, but it raises a valid question. Do our actions really demonstrate that our trust is in God? A lot of times, we confess with our mouths that we trust God and our faith is in him, but our actions speak otherwise. I have been guilty of that, too. It is contradictory to say, "I fully trust God to connect me with a partner," but jump at an opportunity to go on a date without even praying or seeking God's direction first. Once we make the decision to trust God for our answer or solution, our opinions and understanding effectively become null. We become totally dependent on God, asking for direction and actually being still in his presence so he can give us a response.

Often, we are quick to make moves based on what we feel is right in the moment. Somehow, right when we are really trusting God for something, many imitations that seem like the perfect answer to our requests begin to show up. It takes intentionality and discernment to know if an answer truly is from God. He is not an author of confusion, so peace accompanies an answer that comes directly from him.

Without any doubt, waiting is hard. Waiting is painful, it is uncomfortable, it gets frustrating, and it sometimes leads to anxiety or depression. As horrible as all these sound, waiting is part of living. It is one of life's most unenjoyable but inevitable realities, especially if God has given you a word or promise concerning what you're waiting for and it seems to be taking an eternity to manifest. We wait for our dreams to be realized—to get into a school or specific program or to find a spouse. We wait for children, freedom, justice, clear direction or purpose, financial breakthrough, the return of health, restoration for a marriage or relationship, a lost soul's return to Christ, peace over a situation, and the list goes on. I have realized that everyone, at one point in their lifetime, waits for something, some just longer than others.

The moment we have no needs and absolutely nothing we are trusting or waiting on God for, we lose our dependency on him. We may feel that we can meet our needs by our own strength, but when we have tried that and endured waiting, we are often left with no option other than to turn to the one who is able to do everything. I believe that God sometimes ordains a delay, either to show his sovereignty or to enable something much better than what we've ask for to manifest.

Below are a few of the many examples in the Bible of someone's waiting game. Though these people endured sorrow and pain through their waits, joy always came eventually.

- Abraham and Sarah waited for a son: Genesis 15, Genesis 18:1-15
- Hannah waited for a son: 1 Samuel
- Jacob waited for Rachel: Genesis 29
- Elizabeth and Zachariah waited for John: Luke 1:5-25
- Ruth patiently waited for Boaz: Ruth 1-4
- Joseph persevered through many trials: Genesis 37-46.
- Job waited for his life to be restored: Job 1
- The woman with the issue of blood waited for healing: Mark 5:21-34
- The Man at the Pool also waited for healing: John 5:1-15

Now that we hopefully accept, agree, and understand that waiting is almost inevitable, we have achieved our initial breakthrough. In this phase, we know our desires but accept that we have no control over how or when they will be realized. The moment we think we have all the timelines and plans in place, we have decided that we are the captain of our own ship. Would you rather be the captain of your ship and steer your life in whatever direction pleases you? Or would you like to lay all your thoughts and plans at the feet of Jesus and trust him, the ultimate captain, to steer it in his direction? We always have a choice, and the outcome we get is dependent on the choice we make. Please choose wisely.

Today I have given you the choice between life and death, between blessings and curses. Now I call on heaven and earth to witness the

choice you make. Oh, that you would choose life, so that you and your
descendants might live!

— DEUTERONOMY 30:19 (NLT)

The Password: Faith

Given all that we have talked through, one thing remains sure and constant. There is absolutely nothing God cannot do. There is no mountain he cannot move, no situation he cannot turn around. As long as our plans align with his and our trust is completely in him, we can never end up on the losing side. You may be wondering, "How do I know whether my plans align with his or make sure that they will? The answer is simple, seek him first. Once you have a need, idea, or desire, your first response should be to ask, "Lord, what will you have me do?" Begin to pray concerning the situation and seek direction from God, study the word of God and meditate on it, and have the quietness of mind to be able to properly hear when God gives a response.

Don't be hasty. A lot of times, in our haste and desire for an immediate response, we fail to really hear from God. We want an immediate answer, forgetting that God's timeline and ours could be several seconds, minutes, hours, days, months, or even years apart. If we are truly dependent on God and believe that he is capable of granting our request or directing us through the path to having our desires met, we must be willing to wait for him and hear from him.

To fully experience a move of God, you must have faith. To please God and be in right standing with him, you must have faith. To be a Christian is to have faith.

But without faith it is impossible to please him: for he that cometh to
God must believe that he is, and that he is a rewarder of them that
diligently seek him.

Having faith is believing in and trusting Jesus, and this requires knowledge, having conviction, and trusting in him wholeheartedly. Where faith is, fear and doubt cannot exist. They are like light and darkness, which cannot coexist in the same space. Fear is the complete opposite of faith. To be made righteous with God, we must have faith, believing even if we cannot see.

We can find perfect examples of Faith in Hebrews 11. This is one of the chapters of the Bible I have fallen in love with. It is a faith booster, all the doses of faith shots you need to get through any situation or waiting period. Abel gave his best offering by faith, Enoch was taken up to heaven by faith, Noah built an ark by faith, Abraham was ready to sacrifice Isaac by faith, Moses' parents hid him for three months after his birth by faith, the Israelites brought down the wall of Jericho by faith, the prostitute Rahab was spared because of her faith, and the examples go on and on.

The list of faith examples cannot be complete without giving honor to the godfather of faith, the one who the Bible says was made righteous because of his faith, our granddaddy Abraham. His faith is so impressive that it would make an excellent daily prayer point. "Lord, may I have the faith of Abraham all the days of my life." Abraham was made righteous by God and called the Father of Faith because of his display of unwavering trust in God during the most daunting circumstances.

Even when there was no reason for hope, Abraham kept hoping— believing that he would become the father of many nations. For God had said to him, "That's how many descendants you will have!" And Abraham's faith did not weaken, even though, at about 100 years of age, he figured his body was as good as dead—and so was Sarah's womb.

Abraham never wavered in believing God's promise. In fact, his faith grew stronger, and in this he brought glory to God.

— ROMANS 4:18-20 (NLT)

Wow! Isn't that mind-blowing? God is the same yesterday, today, and forever, so by having faith in him, we, too, can have anything we desire and more. Clearly, having faith in God is to our advantage. I urge you to study Romans 4, the entire chapter.

Remember Jesus's disciple Peter? He had faith, you know. He fixed his eyes on Jesus, was not afraid, and what did he do? He walked on water! Then, he faced a slight distraction. Peter shifted his focus from Jesus to the wind. That brought about fear, and Peter began to sink.

But Jesus immediately said to them: "Take courage! It is I. Don't be afraid."

"Lord, if it's you," Peter replied, "tell me to come to you on the water."

"Come," he said.

Then Peter got down out of the boat, walked on the water and came toward Jesus. But when he saw the wind, he was afraid and, beginning to sink, cried out, "Lord, save me!"

Immediately Jesus reached out his hand and caught him. "You of little faith," he said, "why did you doubt?"

And when they climbed into the boat, the wind died down.

Then those who were in the boat worshiped him, saying, "Truly you are the Son of God."

— MATHEW 14:27-33 (NIV)

This story of Peter is one of my favorite examples of the distractions that can bring about fear and obstruct our faith. Distractions can come in the form of friends, family members, or the other people we surround ourselves with. Some people knowingly or unknowingly can suck faith out of you and replace it with fear. When you share your situation with such people, rather than encouraging you and lifting your spirit, they give you every reason why your desired result is impossible. They are negative and describe scenarios of people in your situation who never had a breakthrough. They are readily available to sympathize with you but never have a solution, pray with you, or encourage you with God's word. Please beware of such people. Surround yourself with people who will charge you up, boost your faith, encourage you, and join their faith with yours. Those are the caliber of people you need around you, not just during your waiting period, but always.

Be intentional about what you feed your mind and what you allow through your senses. For example, if you are trusting God for a child, you don't want to feed your mind with stories of people who are barren, read content on miscarriages, or focus on anything else that details the opposite of the healthy child or pregnancy you are trusting God for. Instead, read, watch, and learn about people who have been successful, prepare yourself to be an excellent parent, envision your life as a parent, and begin to plan toward being that person. Do not entertain fear or consume content that substitutes your faith with fear. You must be intentional, and your eyes must remain fixed on Jesus.

> *Looking unto Jesus the author and finisher of our faith; who for the joy that was set before him endured the cross, despising the shame, and is set down at the right hand of the throne of God.*
>
> — HEBREWS 12:2 (KJV)

I have come to understand that faith is a choice of the mind. Basically, it's a state where you condition yourself and your mind to see, live, and believe as if the desire of your heart has actualized, even before it becomes a reality. I'm not saying to create a false reality for yourself or live a lie, but to understand that the mind is a powerful tool that can propel you to push ahead until your dreams become a reality. If you do not condition your mind to function that way, you could miss out on a lot of great things, simply because you did not have faith strong enough to keep you going until your desire became reality. There is a blessing associated with believing in the magnificent power of Jesus, even before seeing.

Then Jesus told him, "Because you have seen me, you have believed; blessed are those who have not seen and yet have believed."

— JOHN 20:29 (NIV)

Where there is doubt, miracles cannot happen, and you are prevented from reaching your maximum potential. When you have faith, there is nothing you cannot do. Your thoughts, actions, and speech are the biggest indications of your faith, so they should not contradict each other.

Imagine, for instance, a person trusting God for a job. He finds a position he feels he's a great fit for, If he's a person of faith, he will take it to God in prayer, thank the Lord for the opportunity that has presented itself, and ask for direction. If he has peace to do so, he'll apply for the position and go through the appropriate process, trusting that if it is God's will, he will get the job. He thanks the Lord in advance for the job, sees himself functioning in that role, and even prepares to start the job—mapping his commute and figuring out how to add value and be an asset to that team. Generally, he behaves as though he got the offer already. That's how he convinces himself and shows God that he knows God can grant him the job. Even though he feels qualified, he admits that his qualifications alone may not suffice, because there could be other candidates more qualified. But he trusts that the grace of God upon his life can make him qualified even where he could be less so.

That's what faith looks like. Everything you say and do shows that you are guided by a higher authority, who is Christ. Be prepared to look foolish to those who don't fully understand the logic of faith. Sometimes, displaying and applying faith may not make sense to the ordinary world. It may feel weird or even stupid, but the things of the spirit sometimes look that way to us, but they are refreshing to God.

For the message of the cross is foolishness to those who are perishing, but to us who are being saved it is the power of God.

— 1 CORINTHIANS 1:18 (NIV)

Contrary to our example of seeking a job by faith, a person without faith or with wavering faith would spend most of his time and energy questioning whether he is a good fit for the job, wondering if there may be better candidates, fretting about all the what-ifs, and focusing on negativity instead of the positive outcomes God is capable of giving. When we apply our faith, it is unnecessary and counterproductive for us to concern ourselves with *if* or *how*. God will carry out what we have committed into his hands. Faith is letting go and letting God.

He replied, "Because you have so little faith. Truly I tell you, if you have faith as small as a mustard seed, you can say to this mountain, 'Move from here to there,' and it will move. Nothing will be impossible for you."

— MATTHEW 17:20 (NIV)

It is incumbent on us to train our hearts and minds to remain focused on all the possibilities that God can and will accomplish. Is this difficult? Yes! I will be the first to admit that there have been many times when I have questioned and wondered while claiming to let God handle it. At the same time, I tried every way possible to figure it out on my own. This is why intentionality is required.

Even when our hearts and minds drift away, we can retrace our way back to the one who makes all things possible. We must continue to remind ourselves that there is nothing God cannot do. Learn to accept the fact that he may not always do things when we want, where we want, or even how we want, but if our requests and desires are in accordance with his will, he will most definitely bring them to pass.

Never forget that one of God's love languages is faith! He inhabits our praise, he loves our gratitude, he delights in our dance and all the fruits of the spirit we exhibit. All of these are important and should not be neglected, but our total faith and trust in God are the crowning jewels. In doing this, we are guaranteed that we are pleasing him, since it is through faith that we please God.

Now, you may be asking, "What if I had faith, didn't doubt or question God, did things that seem foolish as an act of faith, turned deaf ears to negativity, and remained fully focused on God's ability to grant my request, but the answer never came? Or worse, I got the opposite of my request?" Trust me, I have been there. I have cried and asked why. I believe it is okay to feel down when it seems like God isn't coming through after we have done all the right things. The only conclusion I have come to on that is, God is and forever will be God. Why some things just never happen, I honestly don't know and probably will never understand. In some cases, we eventually get to see what God was shielding us from, we get something even better than what we were asking for, or we come to understand that God had a different path for us. Things do somehow work together for our good, just maybe not how we'd hoped.

As a reminder, we should also ask ourselves, "Are my requests or pressing desires in alignment with God's plans and desires for me?" Sometimes, when we pray and do all the right things but seem to not get any answers, it is because we are asking for the wrong thing or the motives behind our requests are selfish. Are your requests motivated by love? I remember a message by Pastor Creflo Dollar in which he said, "if you are not seeing desired results from your prayers, check your motive."

I found this statement profound. I also don't think it's realistic to expect that God will answer requests that stem from negativity or if we have no true connection to him. We would be hypocrites if we prayed constantly for something but never really connected with God and built a relationship with him. Also, we may not see results if we are praying to God to do what he has asked us to do ourselves, or praying for him to do what he has already done in another form. Our connection and relationship with him will help us identify what needs to change as we make our requests known to him.

> *Ye ask, and receive not, because ye ask amiss, that ye may consume it upon your lusts.*
>
> *Ye adulterers and adulteresses; know ye not that the friendship of the world is enmity with God? Whosoever therefore will be a friend of the world is the enemy of God.*
>
> — JAMES 4:3-4 (KJV)

If our prayers have selfish motives or are driven by pride, the probability of God answering them is zero. Communicate with your Heavenly Father with the right motives, and with a totally clear conscience, and he will surely come through.

There is also the flipside, where nothing happens and we just don't understand why. That's where I encourage you to not dwell on or wallow in sorrow or disappointment. Consider this: If God did nothing for you at all, would you still love him? Would you still serve him? Would you still trust him? Do you love him just because of what you expect him to do for you, or because of who he is? Some things, we may never understand. After all, the moment we begin to understand God, he ceases to be God. The reality is, he is able to do all things, and that means he can choose and do as he pleases. Even when we don't understand, we should still trust him.

To fully enjoy and experience God in all of his mightiness, exhibit faith, and live in the goodness he offers, you must accept Jesus into your life. All these testimonies, miracles, signs, and wonders mean nothing if your relationship with Christ is one-sided. If you have not accepted Jesus as your Lord and savior, it is not too late. This moment is a perfect time to do it. He loves you recklessly and would want nothing more than to hear you declare him as Lord over your life. Also, if you have confessed him as your Lord before but have fallen off track, you can rededicate your life to Jesus. It is very simple. Please say this prayer with me:

Lord Jesus, I believe you are the Son of God, and that you died on the cross to rescue me from sin and death and to restore me to the Father. I repent of all unrighteousness and accept you as Lord and savior over my life. I choose you. I give myself to you. Fill me with your spirit. In Jesus's name, amen.

If you said this prayer, I rejoice with you. I congratulate you and welcome you to the family of Christ. It does not end here, and I would love to walk through this journey of discovering Christ with you. Please send an e-mail to yimikaawujoola@ gmail.com, and together, we will build one big Christ-centered family.

Gratitude

An attitude of gratitude is one we should possess at all times. We shouldn't be thankful only when our requests have been met or when we seem to have gotten all we ask for. We often become ungrateful and forget the things God has done for us the moment we encounter a disappointment. There are so many things God does for us every single day that we don't even think to ask him for. We are able to make all these requests—asking God for money, a spouse, kids, health, and all the great things we desire—because we actually have *life*. We don't spend a lot of time expressing gratitude for life, though we can't buy it or work for it. Yet, though we don't think to thank God for it, he freely gives it to us. God made the ultimate sacrifice of sending his only son so that we could be saved, free from sin, and so we can enjoy abundant life.

> *The thief does not come except to steal, and to kill, and to destroy. I have come that they may have life, and that they may have it more abundantly.*
>
> — JOHN 10:10 (NKJV)

> *For God so loved the world, that he gave his only begotten Son, that whosoever believeth in him should not perish, but have everlasting life.*
>
> — JOHN 3:16 (KJV)

As long as we have life, we are able to hope, have faith, and trust God for all our needs. For that, we should always be grateful. I am well aware that it sometimes really is a sacrifice to give praise and thanks, especially when we are down or when we feel like he let us down. We may feel like God has deserted us or doesn't really care about our needs. But we have a choice, to maintain an attitude of praise or wallow and ensure that nothing changes. In the situations where I have made a determination to give praise and thanks regardless of what I'm going through, I have experienced a drastic change in my heart, and my focus suddenly shifts from my troubles to him. I regain my strength and find myself enjoying his peace.

Feeding my mind with God's words has always reminded me of his sovereignty, power, and endless possibilities. This really stirs up a heart of praise and gratitude. Many nights when I felt low while trusting God for my husband, I would play the song "Praise Is What I Do" by William Murphy on repeat. There were times when I felt I had done everything I could possibly do to get a reaction from God, and it seemed nothing was happening. Though I felt so weary and defeated, this song had a way of lifting my spirit and changing the posture of my heart to one full of gratitude. The second verse of the song says:

> Praise is what I do
> Even when I'm going through
> I've learned to worship You
> No my circumstance
> Doesn't even stand a chance
> My praise outweighs the bad
> I vow to praise You Through the good and the bad
> I'll praise You Whether happy or sad
> I'll praise You in all that I go through
> Because praise is what I do
> 'Cause I owe it all to You.

A grateful heart not only lifts our burdens and enables us to enjoy God's peace, but God feeds off our praise. Just as our faith ranks high as his love language and the password to getting into his heart, so does our thanks.

Give thanks in all circumstances; for this is the will of God in Christ Jesus for you.

— 1 THESSALONIANS 5:18 (ESV)

The Lord is my strength and shield.
  I trust him with all my heart.
  He helps me, and my heart is filled with joy.
  I burst out in songs of thanksgiving.

— PSALMS 28:7 (NLT)

God has required a heart of praise and thanksgiving from us, and for all he does, even the things we can't see, the absolute least we could give him in return is gratitude. In all circumstances, our utmost priority should be to praise him— whether just saying "Thank you, Lord," worshiping him with our praise by singing or dancing, testifying of his goodness, or just constantly being appreciative of all he's done. Sometimes, it may be difficult to find the right words to offer, especially when things don't seem to be panning out how we'd anticipated, but it's not complicated at all. A simple, "Thank you, Jesus" will do.

Lord, for all you've done for me, my family, friends, and all that concerns me; for all you are yet to do; for all the work you do behind the scenes; for all I can see and all I cannot see; my heart bursts with gratitude and appreciation to you. From the depth of my heart and the core of my soul, I say a very big "thank you, lord!"

It's a Wrap

They say, "All's well that ends well." I pray that my story has been encouraging to you. It is proof that God makes all things beautiful in their time, and he makes them perfect, too.

I am blessed to be married to Sanmi. My heart beams with joy and gratitude that I get to spend the rest of my life with a man so wonderful, so loving, so caring, so nurturing, so patient, so generous, and so God-loving. I thank God that my reality has been totally different from the negative tales I have heard about the early years of marriage. I can truthfully say that I am thoroughly enjoying my marriage. I can testify of this because Sanmi is God's will for my life. If I hadn't married him, this might be a different story. For the immense mercy and kindness God has shown, I am grateful, and the wait was entirely worth it!

Whatever you are trusting God for, though it has tarried, wait for it. When God turns things around, it will be like a dream...a wonderful dream that has become your reality.

The Bible says that where two or more gather, God is present in their midst. I would like to join my faith with yours as we pray, agree, and decree together in the name of our Lord and savior, Jesus Christ. Let us pray:

Lord Jesus, I thank you for giving me a story to tell and the privilege to share the wonderful testimony of how you have turned my life around for good, all to the glory of your name.

I thank you for my brothers and sisters who have read this story. We gather to say thank you for being a wonderful father to us.

Thank you for loving us so much and for making the ultimate sacrifice for our salvation.

Lord, I join my faith with that of my brothers and sisters and ask that you daily renew faith in the hearts and minds of every one of us.

I ask, Lord, that you increase our faith and trust in you.

As our faith is renewed, we trust that there is absolutely nothing we ask, according to your will and in the name of Jesus, that will not be granted.

Lord, we declare that we believe in you, we believe in your word, and we trust in the power of the name of your precious son, Jesus Christ.

We are confident that, because you are for us, nothing and no one can stand against us.

We submit to your perfect will for our lives and trust that you have our best interests at heart, regardless of what we desire.

We thank you for loving us unconditionally, and from today on, we let go of all that we are and surrender to you alone.

In Jesus's name, amen.

Congratulations!

It is with joy in my heart that I congratulate you on the bountiful miracles God has done and all he will do in your life:

Congrats on your newfound relationship with Christ and the salvation of your soul!

Congrats on your divine connection with your God-ordained spouse, the restoration of broken relationships, your divine and total healing, your new job, the arrival of your healthy bouncing babies, the launching of your business or book, your financial breakthrough, your newfound peace in Christ, your deliverance, the eradication of all your debt, your immigration settlement, your new home, your new car, your graduation, your promotion, your ministry, the souls won for God's kingdom, your new church building, and/or crushing your goals!

On all the marvelous things the Lord will bring to manifestation in your life, I say a big congratulations to you!

PHOTOS

I hope you'll enjoy these photos from key events mentioned in the book.

Friendsgiving

Our Engagement

Our Traditional Wedding

Our Church Wedding

Our First Home

ACKNOWLEDGMENTS

My biggest gratitude goes to God Almighty for choosing and using me as a vessel to share this story of faith. I owe it all to him.

It takes a village, they say. I could not have pulled off writing this book without the love, support, and encouragement of my friends and family. I'm thankful to be surrounded by people who have, in one way or another, blessed and impacted my life.

Special thanks goes to the Adetifa family. To Tosin—who meticulously dissected this book and pointed out every *I* not doted and *T* not crossed—I am grateful to have you in my corner, always thinking ahead on how to make anything I do a success and always being at my beck and call. Thanks for being involved in every monumental part of my life. To Tosin's dearest little girls, Testimony and Love, who are always there to celebrate with their Auntie Yimi. Thank you, Tessy, for always telling me how proud you are of me and how you cannot wait to see me on YouTube. You are the brightest six-year-old ever. And of course, thank you to the daddy of the house, Moyo, for being there to capture every milestone leading to this book.

To my cousins, Tomi and Miriam, who constantly reminded me that my story was worth sharing, your eagerness to read this book kept me on my toes. Thank you.

To my church family, I cannot mention every single member, but I am grateful to belong to such a wonderful, loving, and supportive family.

To my amazing editor, Bridgett Powers, I am so thankful

God chose you for this project. Working with you has been nothing short of wonderful, and I'm sure nobody could have done it better. Thank you for your kind and encouraging words through it all and for working on it wholeheartedly, as unto the Lord. It is apparent that Christ is at the center of all you do.

To every reader of this book, I thank you. If you didn't read this book, then it would have failed. Thank you for joining and supporting me in doing God's work and fulfilling his purpose on my life.

ABOUT THE AUTHOR

Olayimika Awujoola, fondly called Yimi, is first and foremost a child of God. She is a wife to an amazing husband and a mother to a lovely little girl. She is also an author, a speaker, and a project manager by profession.

Yimi is a firm believer in the institution of marriage as ordained by God and has now dedicated her life to helping propel people to Godly, enjoyable, Christian relationships and marriages. She does this by sharing her personal story and communicating the truths from God's word on how relationships should be handled.

Yimi strives daily to be an encourager, a great listener, a prayer partner, and an inspiration to everyone she comes in contact with. Those who know her will tell you she is fun, loving, and caring, and that she has a great sense of humor and an upbeat personality.

She also enjoys planning events, values spending time with

family, and loves to travel. One of Yimi's aspirations is to travel to all the countries in the world, if Jesus tarries.